NOT TO MENTION
THE WAR

Not to Mention the War

by E L M E R   D A V I S

Essay Index Reprint Series

BOOKS FOR LIBRARIES PRESS
FREEPORT, NEW YORK

STANDARD BOOK NUMBER:

8369-1602-6

LIBRARY OF CONGRESS CATALOG CARD NUMBER:

71-107692

PRINTED IN THE UNITED STATES OF AMERICA

IN MEMORIAM

GUY HOLT

CONTENTS

PREFATORY NOTE

These observations, published at sundry times and in divers magazines (most of them in *Harper's*) are here assembled because a few people wanted them in easily accessible form; and in the hope that other people may like to read about matters not immediately connected with the troubles of the times. Yet it seems to have been impossible for one who has been in various forms of the news business for the past twenty-five years (most of my novels, even, in the days when I wrote novels, were pretty largely editorial commentary) to keep entirely away from current interests. I had meant to call this volume *Not to Speak of Hitler,* and then discovered that I had been unable not to speak of the principal fact of our era, even in discussion of quite different matters; and no doubt the archaeologist of the future, in the unlikely contingency that this book should survive other records of the time, could discern from its contents that a war was going on. But I hope it does not obtrude.

No attempt has been made to bring most of these essays up to date, except for the elimination of passages that might connect them specifically with some period of a past that now begins to blur. Some of them, if written as of today, would have to take note of a good deal of material more recently brought to light; none of the conclusions would be substantially different but the topic might have to be approached from a different angle. An exception is the discussion of Wagner, of which extensive revision was necessitated by recent disclosures of the nature of his influence on Hitler; and some of the remarks on the "logic" of history are also subject to qualification in the light of subsequent evidence. No bad guesses have been eliminated in the revision; but this material happened to include few guesses, good or bad. I hope it may briefly distract the customer's mind from current griefs, and perhaps help him recharge his spiritual batteries.

ELMER DAVIS

New York—New Year's Day, 1940

The "Logic" of History

THE "LOGIC" OF HISTORY

IN the Bible of one of the currently most militant
religions it is written: "Our theoretical conclusions
are in no way based on ideas or principles that have
been invented or discovered by this or that would-be
universal reformer. They merely express, in general
terms, actual relations springing from a historical movement going on under our very eyes." In other words,
we are not offering you man-made doctrines which
might be erroneous, but absolute truth. How it was
revealed to the prophets is not stated—a somewhat illogical omission, since there is no evident reason why Karl
Marx and Friedrich Engels should have been less fallible than other would-be universal reformers; but with
that exception the Communist Manifesto, in its interpretation of the present and the future by the logic of
the past, is a document of the same type as the Book of
Deuteronomy or St Peter's sermon on the Day of
Pentecost. Every religion in the day of its vigor boasts
that its doctrines are also scientific truth, revealing to
the faithful the predetermined destiny of mankind.

The tendency is peculiarly strong today. During the war of 1914-18 ecclesiastics predicted that humanity, chastened by tribulation, would turn back to religion; and they were right. They were mistaken only in confusing religion with Christianity. The religions to which men turned to find stability in a shattered world were non-theistic—Communism, Fascism, Nationalism; consequently their interpretations of history are set forth not as revelation but as scientific inductions. Especially the Marxians claim that their religion is not a religion, but a science, and the only science; a good talking-point in an age which likes to believe that it thinks scientifically (and is in fact a good deal farther from so thinking than the abused Victorians). "The highest task of humanity," wrote Lenin, "is to comprehend the objective logic of the economic evolution, with the purpose of adapting the social consciousness to it."

This is a precept which any scientist would approve: find out the facts and then behave accordingly. But when Lenin became boss of Russia, people had to comprehend the logic of economic evolution the way he comprehended it and adapt their social consciousness to his interpretation, not their own; otherwise they were shot. It is a curious sort of science which announces, upon reaching a certain point, that its conclusions are final and unalterable; and enforces their acceptance with machine guns.

For those who can swallow it, however, the Marxian interpretation of history (or any other which is accepted by faith, as beyond revision) is a powerful stimulant. The actual trend of human progress has been discovered by dispassionate investigation; and those who perceive it may hasten by their efforts the working out of the pre-destined Plan. When the Christians, says Gibbon, became convinced that Constantine was God's choice for the imperial throne, "their warm and active loyalty exhausted in his favor every resource of human industry." Logically it might be supposed that Omnipotence was in no need of human aid; but psychologically it does not work out that way. Churches such as the Hardshell Baptists, who believed that if God chose to save the world He would do so without the feeble assistance of contributors to foreign missions, dwindle and die; while creeds that hold, in substance if not in explicit theory, that God helps those who help themselves have a better chance of inheriting the future. The Reverend Professor Reinhold Niebuhr, in his recent *Reflections on the End of an Era,* observes that interpretations of history, if taken seriously, "tend to verify themselves because they direct the course of history to an imagined inevitable goal. . . . The moral imagination finds exactly that meaning in the facts which will make the impossible seem possible."

Even when the impossible must be recognized as impossible by the scientific eye, the moral imagination can find a way out. This teleological interpretation of history was invented by Jewish thinkers of what is known as the Deuteronomic school. They too would have called it objective science, if such a concept had existed in their day; they thought they knew why Israel had fallen and Judah had been chastened, and what measures had to be taken to prevent anything of the sort from happening again. Their formula proved inadequate; King Josiah got right with God, but Pharaoh Necho of Egypt hired some Greeks to fight for him, and that was the end of Josiah. Did this disturb the prophets? Not at all. With admirable fidelity to their convictions and indifference to the evidence, they amended their theory so that it would somehow cover everything if you did not look too closely, and made it stick with the Chosen Remnant who became orthodox Judaism.

The greatest of later Hebrew prophets, St Paul and Karl Marx, broke away from orthodoxy to found religions of their own; but their followers emulate the Exilic writers in explaining away the facts rather than give up the interpretation. On the eve of the triumph of Christianity, Lactantius ("much more perspicuous and positive," Gibbon comments, "than becomes a discreet prophet") set forth this attractive picture: "If the Only God were worshipped there would be no dissensions and wars; no treacheries, frauds, or plunderings; no adultery and prostitution. . . . There would be no need of so many and such diverse laws for ruling men, no need of jails, or armed guards, or the fear of punishment; for to man's perfect innocence the single law of God would be sufficient." Unfortunately it did not work out that way; but the truly faithful were unshaken by the persistence of vice and crime, or even by the unprecedented misfortunes that presently befell the Empire. Augustine, supplemented by Orosius, set himself to explain it all away; whatever you think of the *City of God* as an interpretation of history or as a moral and intellectual influence on subsequent generations, it is certainly one of the most magnificent efforts of the human spirit to transcend an intolerable emotional situation. And it worked, not only for Augustine but for other people; Augustine's structure became part of the foundation of the medieval Church, and Orosius's interpretation of history was still a force in politics when Orosius had been dead twelve hundred years.

The heathen were less hardy. With the rise of Roman power there grew up that interpretation of history which found its noblest expression in the sixth book of the *Aeneid;* the gods had destined Rome to rule the nations. That faith survived till Rome was tottering; even in the fifth century there were stubborn pagans who insisted that the disasters of the Empire were a punishment of apostasy. But the masses refused to follow them in this not illogical view. Why? Because they lacked faith in the major classical deities—faith of the sort that animated the Christians to insist, in the midst of catastrophe, that the judgments of the Lord are true, and righteous altogether. The god whose followers could ignore the evidence was the god who got the converts.

So today. In modern times there has grown up a tendency to look for a logic in history on purely secular grounds. The building up in the physical sciences of a body of ordered knowledge, however incomplete, the discovery of laws valid for the evidence now available, encouraged the hope that the same thing might be done with history. But recent events suggest that more can be done in this direction with faith than with science. It is now the fashion to abuse the bourgeois liberals, optimistic and rationalistic, who believed that the prophet Darwin had discovered a principle which explained history as well as biology. The tendency of evolution was upward; every day in every way we were growing better and better, even if not so rapidly as could be wished.

Anybody can throw mud at those outmoded pagans now, and most of them meekly accept the chastisement. What was their crime? They rested their faith on the evidence, and the preponderance of evidence at present available is against them. So they beat the breast in abased contrition; and more and more of them fly for refuge to one or another of the modern creeds whose

devotees are never disturbed by anything so trivial as
facts which might suggest that they are wrong.

II

All very good if you call it faith; but if you call it
science it must submit to the test of science. Can it
withstand the force of negative instances? I know of no
interpretation of history that can.

This is not an attempt to prove that there is no logic
in history, whether of the Marxian type or any other.
Marx analyzing economic data was a very different person from Marx letting off the apocalyptic hallelujahs of
the Communist Manifesto and the finale of the first
volume of *Capital;* and the creed of economic determin-
ism, as classically stated in the preface to the *Critique
of Political Economy* ("the mode of production of material life determines the *general* character of the social,
political, and spiritual processes of life") is much more
modest and plausible than its embellishments by later
commentators, some of whom have been as perspicuous,
positive, and indiscreet as Gibbon found Lactantius.

Even so, I do not think the evidence at present available is sufficient to support the Marxian interpretation,
or any other which presents itself, explicitly or implic-
itly, as science. There may be a logic in history or there
may not; but at present, except in local and minor in-

stances, such a logic can be discerned only by the eye of faith. Granted that the analysis of historical motivation is often impossibly difficult. Sometimes the evidence is lacking, or (worse) some vital and unsuspected piece of evidence. There is always a deviation due to the position of the observer—as a man in a moving airplane, of whose direction and speed he was as uncertain as we are of the direction and speed of our times, would have trouble in judging the direction and speed of another moving airplane. Moreover, historical events are both effects and causes; and without going so far as some of the physicists who have lately doubted causality or have said that the cause may be subsequent to the effect, it is often impossible to untangle the complex.

All of this is no reason for not trying to figure it out as well as we can. I am only an amateur historian and I do not think that even the ablest professional really knows much about the direction and power of what are called "historical forces"—social, economic, or spiritual. But whatever those forces amount to, the record will show that at certain critical moments they have been deflected, and with decisive effect, by something to which at present we can give no better name than Chance. Chance and what is perhaps a subdivision of Chance— Personality.

As factors in history these are certainly no new dis-

coveries. Even Marx conceded that "the acceleration and
retardation of the general process of development depend to a considerable degree on accidents, among which
figure the character of the persons at the head of the
movement." This is an admission which some of his
followers, even those in the apostolic succession, might
well take to heart. The Communist revolution was supposed to occur first in Germany, or England; why, in
fact, did it occur in Russia? Stalin's explanation (*Foundations of Leninism,* pp. 83-86—English translation)
seems to me very weak. The most logical reason is one
which he omits altogether—that the severe repressive
measures of Imperial Russia drove more and more of
the abler radicals into the extreme revolutionary party,
and compelled that party to submit to a rigorous and
salutary self-discipline if it was to hold together at all.
Beyond that there was one completely illogical reason,
by any present concept of logic: the leaders of that party
at the critical moment happened to be a couple of men
named Lenin and Trotzky.

There was also, while we are in those geographical
regions, a man named Genghis Khan. Where does he
fit into the logic of history? Marx might say that such a
character and such a career were the logical consequences
of the nomadic mode of production. But there had been
none comparable to it in nomad history before him; and
with all respect to Tamerlane, there has been none quite

comparable since. Where is the logic in the fact that the backwash of men displaced by his conquests, using the military technique learned from his armies, uprooted the apparently stable residuary conquests of the Crusaders? Where, for that matter, is the logic in the turning aside of his armies when they had the much admired civilization of thirteenth-century Europe at their mercy? Possibly they found the wooded and hilly landscape of much of Central Europe uncongenial to the nomadic mode of production; but it was the usual custom of the Mongols to let their local subjects do the producing, while they lived on the product, like members of the Tammany organization.* And certainly the effects of the Mongol conquest on the social, political, and spiritual processes of the life of Asia and of Eastern Europe were more considerable for several centuries than those of the mode of production.

About the end of the eighteenth century there was

---

* Colonel Moravec of the late Czechoslovak General Staff has offered a more plausible explanation. "Grass," he says, "is the gasoline of the horse"; and in forested mountain countries the Mongols could not find enough of this fuel to keep their cavalry going. Yet in Bohemia, still more in Hungary, there must have been plenty of grass in the thirteenth century. The Mongols, after all, were peculiar men; and quite possibly the simplest version of the story is true—that they got word that the Great Khan was dead and his successor wanted them to come back home.

beginning in England a decisive change in the mode of production. That influenced the social, political, and spiritual processes of subsequent generations, up to and including our own; but along with it went the influence of a simultaneous event known as the French Revolution, and of the occurrences that grew out of it. One of these occurrences was a man named Napoleon Bonaparte, whose consequences have by no means passed away. It is true enough that Napoleon was a product of his age; if he had been born fifty years earlier he could hardly have risen to be any more than a general of artillery in the "temperate and indecisive conflicts" of the eighteenth century. But from 1799, certainly from 1804, the age was largely a product of Napoleon. How did Napoleon get to the top? The times were ripe for the coup d'état of the 18th Brumaire; if you like, it was compelled by the logic of history. But how did it happen that General Bonaparte made it, and no one else? General Masséna might have made it, but he had no political ambition; General Moreau might have made it, but he was hesitant and politically inept. As for General Bonaparte, the 18th Brumaire was notoriously the weak moment of his career; as Curzio Malaparte puts it, the only difference between the Napoleon of that day and the bungling failure Boulanger was Lucien Bonaparte. Is it logical that Napoleon, at the one moment when he faltered, should have had a brilliant brother who was in a position to pull him through—a brother who soon became disinclined to help him further?

Subsequent European history would have been very different if a less restless man, a Moreau or a Masséna, had made that coup d'état instead of General Bonaparte—American history too, for without the renewed war with England, France might have chosen to fight for Louisiana rather than sell it. Subsequent history, both European and American, would for that matter have been very different if Napoleon had paid serious attention to Robert Fulton and his far from impracticable submarine. Leo Tolstoy defaced the greatest novel ever written with a long-winded argument designed to prove that Napoleon was nothing—the inconsiderable tool of vast impersonal forces. But if Napoleon, during the critical hours of the battle of Borodino, had not been incapacitated by indigestion (or *petit-mal* epilepsy, whichever it was), Borodino might have been a victory as decisive as Jena; and the Russian popular uprising of which Tolstoy was justifiably proud might not have given Napoleon much trouble if there had been no Russian army left to serve as its spearhead. A logic which rationalizes the diet of kings would have to be very rigorous indeed.*

---

* But maybe Tolstoy was right about Borodino (though that is far from proving his general thesis). Since this was written

III

An implicit teleological interpretation of history was a commonplace of American patriotism in our early decades; we were God's chosen people, appointed to exemplify the superior merit of republican democracy to all the nations of the earth. But we might never have got started but for the indolence of Sir William Howe, who could always win a battle but lacked the energy to finish a war; but for the fact that Lord George Germain, in his hurry to get off to the country for the week-end, would not stop to send the letter that would have ordered Howe to join Burgoyne; but for Charles Lee, who with the worst of intentions saved his adopted country by persuading Howe to go to the Chesapeake instead; but for Colonel Skene, who for personal reasons induced Burgoyne to take the long hard route through the woods instead of the easy one by Lake George, and thus gave Schuyler time to organize the defense. Nor for that matter if Benedict Arnold had not been the kind of man who insisted on getting into a fight, even when he had

---

the memoirs of Caulaincourt have been published; so we now know that both Berthier and Murat, toward the end of the day, told Napoleon that in view of the immense losses it would be too risky to throw in the Guard for the final stroke that might have completed the victory. If it looked too risky even to Murat—

been ordered to stay out of it; or if Washington had not been Washington. Such a chain of contingencies, every one of them essential, might with some plausibility be called the providence of God; it can hardly be called the logic of history.

Our exemplification of the merits of republican democracy would not have been very effective if this nation had blown up in mid-career; which it might have done but for a man named Abraham Lincoln—a man not naturally very ambitious, who qualified as presidential timber largely because his wife was not only ambitious but shrewish, so that he went out and got a reputation in preference to staying at home; and who got the presidential nomination largely because six years earlier Horace Greeley had quarreled with Thurlow Weed over so trivial a matter as the Lieutenant-Governorship of New York. But for Greeley's vanity and Mary Todd's temper this nation might easily have split in two.

After Lincoln's day the country took a very different turn; its mode of production was changing, and social, political, and spiritual life changed with it. Much of that would doubtless have occurred under any President; but much of what happened almost certainly would not have happened if Booth had missed Lincoln. Lincoln if he had lived would have pursued the policies that Andrew Johnson pursued in vain. No one can surely say that he would not have failed too, if he had tried to oppose the rising tide of passion and interest that turned the South over to carpetbaggers and the North to speculators. But there were differences between Lincoln and Johnson—immensely important differences. In the first place, there was Lincoln's tremendous prestige at the end of the war; Radical Republican newspapers would hardly have dared to lie about him as shamelessly as they lied about Johnson. Also, Lincoln was one of the ablest politicians who ever sat in the White House; his outstanding distinction in an age of violent passions was that he never lost his temper (as Johnson did, to his heavy cost) and never let his vision of what was desirable interfere with his coolly realistic estimate of what was possible.

And one thing more—the whole emotional background would have been different if Lincoln had lived. No one can read the newspapers of April 1865 without being struck with the fact that the universally dominant emotion was simply a feeling of immense relief. There was at first apparent no hatred, no bitterness; a long agonizing ordeal was over, and men on both sides seemed to feel like survivors of a great natural cataclysm who must now forget their old differences and get together to repair the damage. For a few days it appeared that the whole country was ready to proceed to reconstruction with malice toward none, with charity for all.

In some degree, no doubt, that appearance was illusory. Thaddeus Stevens would have been Thaddeus Stevens, and human nature would have been human nature, whether Lincoln lived or died; after men had got used to peace they might have backslid from their momentary virtue. But no slow and normal retrogression could have been anything like the sudden explosive release of suspicion and vindictiveness and hatred that came with the news that Lincoln had been assassinated. Lincoln living could never have had to face the insuperable difficulties that were created by the mere fact of Lincoln dead.

One other instance from domestic history. It is a Marxian doctrine—emotionally, if not logically, the cardinal doctrine of them all—that capitalism is doomed to ultimate destruction by its inherent self-contradictions. Since Marx wrote we have learned that capitalism can stand immense and various modifications without being destroyed; nevertheless those contradictions are troublesome enough to all its varieties, and have been conspicuously troublesome in this country, though with varying intensity, since 1929. Revolution, says Lenin—meaning thorough revolution—is impossible unless there is a crisis which makes not only the "exploited" but the "exploiters" feel that they can no longer go on in the old way. The United States was dangerously near that situation, in emotion if not in underlying fact, in the early summer of 1932. That there was no revolutionary party competent to take advantage of the confusion may have been a logical consequence of American social development. But it is hard to see anything but pure chance in the fact that we touched bottom in a presidential year, when we could change our leadership in the familiar non-revolutionary way; or that the secondary banking crisis, less profound but more acute, came to a head on the very day when the new President took command. No one can say how much trouble we may have been saved by a mere accident of chronology.*

Capitalism may ultimately choke to death on its own contradictions; but there is now going on in this country a desperate effort to iron out some of those contradictions, to repair the machine and make it workable. It is possible that this effort may attain a real and durable success; which, if it happens, will disprove the Marxian reasoning. But what would it prove affirmatively

---

* There is of course a school of thinkers that denies that there was any accident about it. According to their doctrine Republican policies were at last beginning to restore prosperity in the summer of 1932; but the insensate mob, unable to realize what was going on, ruined everything by electing a Democrat and thus destroying that most precious of intangibles, Confidence. After which fear of impending disaster began to knock over the banks, one by one. The evidence offered in support of this theory is unimpressive except to the devout.

about the logic of history? If capitalism is saved in America (however it may have to be modified in the process) it will be saved because there was a President at a certain time, who was nominated because he was a Protestant named Roosevelt, and elected because he was not an incumbent named Hoover. Not a hundred people of the twenty-two million who voted for him could have had any clear idea of what he was and what he was going to do. And after he was elected he lived to take office only because a man who wanted to kill him was a bad shot and hit some other people instead. Providence, if you like; but certainly not logic.

IV

All this may sound like the long discredited "great-man theory" of history, which, says Professor Shotwell, explains nothing. Shotwell is a high authority but Sir Charles Oman, perhaps, is even higher; and he observes (in *On the Writing of History*) that "so far is history from being an impersonal, logical process that there is more truth in the much decried theory of Thomas Carlyle that it has been largely affected by the working of individual men of mark on their contemporaries. . . . Let us never talk of the world stream, or of inevitability, but reflect that the human record is illogical, often cataclysmic." Sometimes it seems that quite as valid as the great-man theory is the small-man theory, the effect on history of the fact that at a given time a position of tremendous importance was occupied by a man (such as Honorius, of whom more presently) who was not big enough for his job. In any case, the accusation that "it explains nothing," damning enough for a theory, is hardly valid as an indictment of facts. In the record of every science there are observations of fact which explained nothing at the time, but served the useful purpose of discrediting mistaken explanations previously prevalent. I do not cite these familiar instances in support of the great-man theory, or any other; only to suggest that Chance plays so large a part that we cannot yet formulate any theory at all that even roughly fits the evidence.

In no field of history has the search for logical explanation been so diligent as in the study of the decline and fall of the Roman Empire. This is the only known instance of the decay of a more or less universal civilization, which might serve as something of an object lesson to our own; accordingly it has been very thoroughly studied, and the attempt to explain it has exercised some of the ablest historians who ever wrote. Almost any preacher or politician can tell you why Rome fell, but the men who know most about it are not so ready with glib explanations. Even they must admit at critical moments the decisive interposition of Chance.

The first question is why Rome did not "fall" much

earlier. In the first century B. C. the civilized Mediterranean world seemed to be disintegrating; but the decline was postponed for two hundred years, the fall for
two hundred and fifty years more. Why? The strength
of the centripetal and constructive forces in society?
Those forces existed, had always existed; but in the
fourth decade before the birth of Christ they were organized and led to victory by a man named Augustus.
And who, in the beginning, was Augustus? Only the
heir of a famous name; a boy, untried and unknown.
The legions of Caesar turned to him, rather than to the
mature and brilliant Antony, because he was Caesar's
heir and nearest legitimate kinsman; nobody could guess,
then, that this young stranger was to become one of the
shrewdest politicians and ablest organizers of all time.

After two centuries the structure built by Augustus
began to decay; or rather the processes of decay, present
in Rome as in every society, became stronger than the
processes of construction. There was a slow social and
economic deterioration, most thoroughly analyzed by
Rostovtzeff (who would be the last to claim that his
analysis is final), and a growing intellectual and spiritual
lassitude, a loss of nerve, which no one has yet adequately
explained. Rostovtzeff thinks that perhaps the chief
trouble was the "economic backwardness" of the Empire;
which might seem to support the doctrine that everything
is conditioned by the mode of production. There was a
costly leisure class; and much too much of the national

income was spent on useless overhead, the embellishment of hundreds of cities. A primitive system of production could not stand the burden and began to crack.

But why was Rome economically backward? There had been a promising beginning of capitalism in the Greek states that succeeded Alexander; it withered chiefly because of the incessant wars, whose motivation was personal and political, not economic. When Rome had stabilized the Mediterranean world, capitalism of a primitive type took hold again; its development was halted partly by the tendency above mentioned to put too much money into temples, theaters, and baths (which sprang from many causes, few of which had any economic aspect); but chiefly by the Roman civil wars, again personal and political in motivation.

Ancient capitalism might have got somewhere if it had used machinery. The later Greeks invented machines, including a steam engine; but they treated them as scientific toys, or at best as weapons in siege warfare. Why? No one can say, except that such was the tendency of the Greek mind.* If capitalism never took hold in antiquity it would seem to be due to a reversal of the Marxian formula: the mode of production was deter-

---

* In the Marxist quarterly *Science and Society* (fall issue 1938) Benjamin Farrington goes into this a little more deeply. Ancient opinion regarded anything that had to be done with the hands—even, in the end, surgery—as beneath the dignity of a gentleman; consequently there was a progressive "divorce

mined by social, political, and spiritual processes. Marx might call this a mere retardation; but a retardation of two thousand years is no small item in the short span of history.

The obvious and proximate cause of Roman decay, as all historians have recognized, was the disastrous civil

---

between theory and practise." Further, the need of machinery was not felt by the owner class on account of the cheapness of slave labor; and the slave had no incentive to invent labor-saving gadgets when he would have had to go on working just as hard, and the extra profit would have gone to his owner.

So far Professor Farrington writes as a classical scholar, and even the profane can follow him; but his explanation of the decay of scientific speculation becomes a doctrinal sermon. "There was an inevitable clash between the spirit of science and the requirements of government"—in republican Rome, in democratic Athens. "The Ionians, free from the problems of government" (because they lived under the Persian despotism) "gave us daring cosmological speculations"; and there was further progress under the autocratic Ptolemies, who "believed in the possibility of using the results of science for administrative purposes." The logical implication, that scientific progress is possible only under a totalitarian dictatorship, is such sound Stalinism that it is perhaps pointless to remark that Ionian speculation began, at least, while Ionia was still free. But on Professor Farrington's reasoning one would expect a glorious flowering of science, both pure and applied, in later Rome—say under Valentinian, when slave labor was no longer cheap and common and the government was despotic enough for any taste. In fact of course there was plenty of speculation in fourth-century Rome, but it all channeled off into doctrinal religion; as it did in contemporary Russia until Stalin liquidated the heretics.

wars between ambitious generals; which were due to a
structural weakness that made the Emperor, in theory an
elected magistrate, in fact the creature of the army. This
might be called a part of the logic of Roman development; Augustus could not have arranged things any
other way. Nevertheless, for a century and a quarter
after 69 A. D. there were no serious civil wars; and in the
latter part of that period Europe was more prosperous
and better governed than it was to be again for seventeen
hundred years, more peaceful than it has ever been since.
Emperor after emperor, in those days, was picked out by
his predecessor as the best man to carry on the job—
chosen, and adopted as a son for greater moral effect.
The first emperors of the series happened to be childless;
the fourth, Antoninus Pius, had two sons who died before he came to power—and a daughter, whom he married to his chosen successor Marcus Aurelius. The
principle of adoption, supported by all the educated
classes, seemed established, and with it the internal
stability of the Empire.

But the wise and virtuous Marcus broke the precedent
and passed on his power to his son Commodus, either a
lunatic or (among other things) a monumental incompetent.* In thirteen years Commodus managed to wreck

---

* Recent writers, notably G. P. Baker, have pointed out that
Commodus, the son of an emperor and the grandson of an
emperor, was a virtually inevitable choice. All the emperors
from Nerva on, says Baker, "had endless worry over the prob-

the constructive work of a century, and left a chaos—
political, financial, and moral—in which the Empire became again, and remained forever after, the prize of the
strongest. Even Rostovtzeff, who knows more than anybody else about the impersonal forces that were at work,
thinks that another two or three strong emperors (such

---

lem of their successor, and all must have realized the element
of pure luck that entered into it. They could not go on indefi-
nitely without children. As soon as one of them had a presentable son, the result was a foregone conclusion."

But Marcus who, though we know him chiefly as a philosopher—again a matter of chance, the loss of most of the trustworthy histories of his reign—was in fact one of the ablest
generals and administrators that Rome ever produced, must
have known what Commodus was and what he would do to the
Empire. The designation of Commodus as his successor, and
the high honor Marcus always showed to his worthless adopted
brother Verus, would indicate either that he was a poor judge
of men—and he seems to have selected very able subordinates—
or else that his high sense of public duty was inoperative inside
the family.

Commodus was so much handsomer than his father, and his
tastes were so different, that then and since scandal has hinted
that his mother had a taste for gladiators. But he was no handsomer than his mother's father, and certainly it is no rare occur-
rence for a son to react against his father's ideas; especially when
the father is a man like Marcus Aurelius. The tone of his
Meditations was no doubt the tone of his domestic conversation
as well; and that worthy work seems to me singularly ill calculated to incline anybody less austere than Marcus to the pursuit
of virtue.

as the adoptive principle had given) might have kept Rome peaceful and fairly prosperous for some scores of years more, with incalculable consequences for the future of civilization.

There followed a century of disintegration, after which some sort of order was reestablished. The new structure built by Diocletian and Constantine was a grotesque caricature of the Empire of Augustus—barbarous, tawdry, and very uncomfortable except for the small class of rich racketeers. Still it was the most imposing state west of China; it fought constantly against one civilized enemy and many barbarians and held them at bay. Then, a century after Diocletian, the western half of it began to collapse. Why?—and why not the eastern half too? Bury, the best authority on this period, points out that decline and fall are two very different matters; the impersonal forces assigned as causes for the one have little to do with the other. In the "fall" of Rome, he thinks, there was no logic at all; it was "the consequence of a series of contingent events."

The irruption of the Huns and the consequent displacement of the barbarian population of Europe might be fitted into a logic of world history, but not of Roman history. Rome gave asylum to the Visigoths, flying from the Huns; and it may be part of the logic of the later Empire that Roman officials who dealt with the Visigoths were grafters like some of our nineteenth-century

Indian agents, and like them provoked an outbreak. The Roman army met the Visigoths at Adrianople; and if it had won there, as it had often won before, there would never have been any fall of Rome. But the Romans lost at Adrianople—because the Emperor Valens was too impatient to wait for reinforcements, and because he was misled by his scouts.

The Emperor Theodosius got the Visigoths back on the reservation, and so long as he lived they stayed there. But he died in middle age and left his empire to two sons (each ruling a half) who were little better than imbeciles. Honorius, the more imbecilic, reigning in Italy, entrusted the government to a German named Stilicho, who for personal reasons neglected opportunities to crush the Visigoths when they took the war path again; and eventually they sacked Rome. So Bury, whose judgment of Stilicho is perhaps harsher than most, but who certainly cannot be accused of not knowing what he is talking about. "It may be said," he observes, "that a German penetration of Western Europe must ultimately have come about. But even if that were certain, it might have happened in another way, at a later time, more gradually, and with less violence." And accordingly with far different consequences.

Meanwhile the eastern half of the Empire somehow managed to pull through. It is usual to explain this as due to the greater prosperity of the East, its older and more deeply rooted culture. But the eastern provinces immediately exposed to the barbarians were poorer and less cultured than Italy and Gaul. About the year 400 a German general dominated Constantinople as other German generals later dominated Rome; yet he was overthrown and killed. Why? The record is obscure; but his fall seems to have been chiefly due to a mere accident which left half of his army within and half outside of the walls at a critical moment. The rest of the story is too long to be recited here; but it looks as if Constantinople survived when Rome fell simply because it got the breaks.

The conversion of Constantine, and the consequent Christianization of the Empire, was an event of enormous importance. Leaving aside the much debated question of whether it did more good than harm to the Church and to the world, let us look for the logic in it. It is the commonest view that Constantine turned Christian from policy; he saw that the Church, though weak in numbers, was strong in spirit, the only institution headed upward in a world where everything else was slipping down. But Christianity was weakest in the provinces where Constantine, before he became emperor, was strongest; his conversion won him friends but also made him enemies; as an act of policy its wisdom is seriously debatable. Accordingly, Church historians and some of the bitterest enemies of the Church have agreed in regarding it as a real conversion—that is, something which happened in the consciousness of Constantine for reasons not related to logic. Even Gibbon, who goes at length into the political advantages and cannot swallow the attendant miracles, will not deny the sincerity of the conversion. Modern psychologists might not question even Constantine's vision of the cross in the sky, seen at a moment of great emotional tension by a soldier who lived in a time of ignorance and superstition.

V

The factor most often overlooked by historical logicians is that of the cumulative consequences; if one great event had happened otherwise, the major outlines of all that followed would have been different. Otherwise, or at another time; the consequences are dependent on the date. The war of 1914 had perhaps been made inevitable by the logic of impersonal forces; but it was not inevitable in 1914. Nobody then wanted a war on that scale; it was the result of the interaction of the mental processes of many men—their emotions, their failures of insight. That war almost happened in 1905, in 1909, in 1911, in 1913; its consequences had it begun in any of those years would have been incalculably different, as they would have been if it had been deferred to 1917 or later. By the end of 1916 the two European alliances

had fought each other to a standstill; the War was decided by the intervention of America, which might have
intervened, but did not, in 1915. Radicals have a dogmatic explanation of all this; but I think anyone who
disinterestedly examines the evidence—Bernstorff's book
above all—should conclude that the reason America did
not fight in 1915 (when we might have lost, and the
consequences even of victory would have been enormously different) and did fight in 1917 was chiefly the state
of mind of Woodrow Wilson, a state of mind in which
logic played a minor part.*

There are other factors that fit no logical scheme. In
the sixteenth century great forces—economic, political,
psychological—were at work to break up the medieval

---

* A good many comparable instances from current history
come to mind, but one is enough. It looks at this writing (November 1939) as if the Allies would have had a much better
chance of stopping Hitler if they had fought him a year sooner.
If the Czechs had refused to accept the Munich dictate and
preferred to go down fighting, public opinion in England and
France would probably have forced the appeasing governments
to support them; but the Czechs decided not to fight—chiefly
because the General Staff concluded that they could not simul-
taneously hold off the Germans in front and the Poles in the
rear. The history of Europe for the next millennium might have
been different if Polish foreign policy had not been conducted,
in September 1938, by the "realist" Colonel Beck, who could
see the end of his own nose so plainly that he was unable to
believe that there was anything beyond it.

world. But the actual results of those forces, the directions in which they were channeled, depended on circumstances whose necessity does not appear. The late Dr. Charles MacLaurin, in his historical essays entitled *Post Mortem,* suggests that England might never have left the Church if the syphilis of Henry VIII had not incapacitated Katharine of Aragon for bearing living children after Mary; and that the triumph of particularism and semi-triumph of Protestantism in Germany was made possible by the gluttony, and consequent arteriosclerosis, of Charles V.

No philosophy of history has room for sexual attraction. Yet its primary and obvious effects have sometimes been important; Roman history would have been different if Caesar, and after him Antony, had not fallen in love with Cleopatra. Far more weighty are the secondary effects—the doings of men and women born from specific unions, who could have been born from no other unions. Letizia Ramolino, a remarkable woman, had eight children—four who were nonentities, three (I include Pauline) who were distinctly superior, and one transcendent genius. What sort of children would she have borne if the traits of her stock had been blended with some other germ plasm than that of Carlo Bonaparte? Whether she picked him out or had him picked for her I do not know, but the destiny of the nineteenth century hung on the choice. If Philip of Macedon, in his younger days, had married any one but the enigmatic barbarian Olympias, he might have been succeeded by a son like himself, who would have consolidated an indestructible kingdom west of the Taurus; instead of a superman who overran the world and then drank himself to death, leaving behind him a Hellenized Orient and the seeds of an Orientalized and Christianized Occident. The marriage of Henry VIII to Anne Boleyn looked at one time like a horrible mistake; yet from it sprang Elizabeth, and modern England.

But no logical interpretation, you protest, could rationalize such factors as these? Exactly; and it is on such factors as these that the actual course of history depends, however the trend may be directed by impersonal forces. In the present state of human knowledge such matters as the marriage of Letizia Ramolino and the appetite of Charles V can be woven into a logical scheme only on the assumption that everything—personal and impersonal, internal and external—is causally related to everything else; that every psychological impulse, as well as every event, is predestined; that nothing that ever happened or ever will happen could have happened otherwise. This may be true; any logician could make out a good argument for it. But as a working hypothesis human nature has never been able, and probably never will be able, to accept it; even Moslems usually act as if what they did or omitted would make a difference.

Pure fatalism is not only not a logic of history; it makes a logic of history impossible. Everything happens because it happens, and that is all.

There is no apparent reason why some day a passably adequate philosophy of history may not be evolved; but that day is remote. "We do not know natural necessity in the phenomena of the weather," wrote Lenin, "and to that extent we are slaves of the weather. Nevertheless, without knowledge of this necessity" (*i.e.* without knowledge of its laws, of what it is) "we know that it exists." True; as we are aware of some sort of law, though we can discern it very dimly, in the run of the cards, the sequence of numbers that turn up on the roulette wheel. We know rather more about the laws of the weather than we did when Lenin wrote the foregoing, twenty-five years ago; we shall learn more about the weather and about human behavior too. Some day we may understand the laws of sexual attraction as a branch of electro-chemistry; we may know why a man eats himself out of an empire. But till we understand the laws of such matters and the probably more complex laws of their interrelation no philosophy of history can be called scientific.

Human behavior, individual and collective, is a more perplexing study than the weather; and its students are more likely to be deflected by emotion, by the impulse to find evidence in support of a faith already held. Mythologies of history, as Niebuhr observes, are pragmatically useful; they encourage the devout. But once adopted they become dogmas, which no man may safely deny. It would be dangerous to question the Hitlerite interpretation of history in Berlin, the Marxian interpretation in Moscow; at sundry times and in divers places it has been dangerous—and may become dangerous again—to question various forms of the Christian interpretation. However, there is this to be said for the people who explain history in terms of the miraculous interpositions of divine Providence—they do not try to harmonize their scheme with the laws of logic; they do not think they give it additional authority by calling it a science.

Prophets at the Crossroads

PROPHETS AT THE CROSSROADS

IN these times of tribulation, when men in Europe and China call on the rocks to cover them, and the great and terrible day of the Lord may be just around the corner for everybody else, the most pertinent of all questions is "What shall we do to be saved?"

Two evangelists from England have lately tried to show us the way of salvation: Mr Hilaire Belloc with *The Crisis of Civilization,* Mr Gerald Heard with *The Third Morality.* Each knows what is the matter with us, and how to cure it. Unfortunately their diagnoses, and their remedies, are utterly different; and the resemblances between the authors only make life harder for the earnest truth seeker. Both Heard and Belloc insist that morality must have a religious sanction, both are rigorously logical, and both belong to the now popular either-or school of thinkers. Civilization, they agree, faces an inexorable alternative, either this or that; but their thisses are irreconcilable and even their thats are not the same. Heard sees civilization headed for collapse and chaos unless it accepts his gospel; to Belloc the alternative to salvation is Communism, a fate worse than death.

Belloc's book is by far the easier reading, and may be more briefly dismissed since his remedy—the return to Catholicism, of course—is a familiar one; you take it or leave it, according to taste. But since he feels that the present crisis is immediately due to economic dislocations (hastened and intensified, but not, he concedes, wholly caused, by the Reformation) he would implement the Catholic philosophy by the economic reforms set forth in his *Restoration of Property*—a recreation of the (possibly somewhat idealized) fifteenth century world of guild industry and peasant-owned farms. The substance of the book was delivered as lectures at Fordham University and naturally in addressing his coreligionists Belloc did not have to offer much argument for the truth and necessity of Catholicism. The reader not already converted will be conscious of the omission. Non-Catholics will differ from many of his interpretations of history, but it must be remarked that he treats the Reformation, and the conditions that produced it, with an objectivity rare and admirable in a partisan of either side.

Not quite so much can be said for his treatment of current affairs. He is sure that the inescapable choice for civilization lies between Catholicism and Communism; Cardinal Faulhaber might see it otherwise. It is fashionable nowadays to treat Protestantism, capitalism, parliamentary democracy, and other dominant factors of the nineteenth century as beneath discussion, but a book which never mentions Fascism can hardly be called a complete picture of the contemporary world. To be sure Catholicism and Fascism get along very well in Spain and Italy; but Belloc says nothing about Italy, and in his brief allusion to the Spanish war he is conscientious enough to mention the Moors, but not the Italians. Is it possible that he is ashamed of the company the Church keeps?

Mr Gerald Heard is even surer than Belloc that unless we be born again we shall not enter into the kingdom of God—so sure that he makes only passing mention of economics, confident that if we seek the Kingdom first, all things else shall be added unto us. This is, he holds, fundamentally a moral and religious crisis, but he dismisses Belloc's solution as no longer possible for thinking men. It was a mere phase of the Anthropomorphic Cosmology which produced the First Morality, the expression of a transcendent Creator's will. That picture of the universe was shattered by the successive blows of Newton, Darwin, and Freud. The destructive effects of *The Origin of Species by Natural Selection* were not at once apparent, because a generation brought up by pious parents retained their ethics, even after the ontological foundation was gone; but the second generation drew the logical conclusion and there followed the Second

or Mechanomorphic Morality, seething with lust and
red in tooth and claw, by which we all now live—at least,
if Mr Gerald Heard is correctly informed. "Ethics," he
says, "must be the logical system of action built up from
such general truths as can be discovered from an unbiased observation of reality." Such observation, by the
dimmer light which shone till lately, indicated a mechanical universe which logically imposed on its inhabitants
a compulsion to unlimited money-grabbing and forni-
cation; this we must do, whether we enjoy it or not, and
(since everyone behaves logically in the world of Mr
Heard) this is what we are all doing. But—glad tidings
of great joy—materialism has now been disproved, the
latest unbiased observations disclose a very different cosmic picture; and on that firm foundation the Third
Morality not only can but must be erected. If not, "what
we have called ethics will disappear and what we have
called civilization will disappear with them." Either, or.

No sane man would hesitate long between such alternatives; but the penitent stumbling down the sawdust
trail finds Mr Heard detaining him. Since all morality
must rest on a cosmological foundation, we must first
learn what happy discoveries about the nature of the
universe, discerned by the latest unbiased observation of
reality, have delivered our souls from error's chain and
made it logically permissible to sleep alone and like it.
We know now that "the universe is simply a vast system

of force-waves," and the world as we apprehend it is a mere mental construct out of such chips and splinters of reality as our senses are able to perceive—material selected under the influence of greed and fear; or, as they put it in India, an illusion based on desire.

Where Heard goes beyond India is in buttressing this view by the latest findings of Occidental science, or some of them. He has not much use for either the senses or the reason—the deeper truths lie in the unconscious; but it appears that scientific evidence which backs him up (unlike that which controverts him) is not a mere fallible selection based on greed and fear. The Principle of Indeterminacy plays a large part in it, and Rhine's experiments in extra-sensory perception, and a good deal of other material on which an unscientific reviewer is not competent to pass judgment. But its meaning is clear to the adept. Mr Heard knows, for instance, that natural selection is only an exploded superstition; what causes the origin of species is cosmic rays from some super-nova, powerful enough to pierce, at intervals, the Heavyside layer. He knows, too, a good deal about what happens on the other side of Jordan—who is and who is not likely to inherit eternal life. He knows, in sum, that the universe is essentially one, that human personalities are "not separate wholes but parts of a single state of being"; and that if we only get rid of craving and try to merge ourselves into the Larger Life, "man may make

any universe up to the standard of which he is prepared
to live. . . . The one fundamental objective fact is that
the energy-radiation will sustain and substantiate any
construction creative desire calls upon it to support and
fulfill." Canst thou bind the sweet influences of Pleiades,
or loose the bands of Orion? Apparently thou canst,
after indoctrination in the Third Morality.

Not even dialectical materialism offers so bright a
prospect of making up your own world as you go along.
If man will only "realize his unity with all life and
being" the troubles of these times will pass away. But a
generation of vipers must be converted, and in the time
of transition it is the duty of the adherent of the Third
Morality to lead the "rationed life," aiming at "efficiency
and innocency." The innocence is not an eremitic virtue; "teams" of the efficient and innocent should be
formed, nuclear cells for the evangelization of the world;
and fortunately a technique is available for the practice
and strengthening of virtue.

Vegetarianism is part of it, not only because it is
wicked to take animal life (though Heard reluctantly
admits that we may have to kill dangerous bacteria till
we can think of some more fraternal way to treat them)
but because "the reflective, controlled type is vegetarian,
the impulsive and impatient is the high-protein eater."
E.g., those patient, non-impulsive vegetarians, Adolf
Hitler and Bernard Shaw. (It is curious that Heard

sanctions, by implication, the eating of beans, abhorrent
to some of his forerunners.) Deep breathing and correct posture, rhythm and the dance, are also conducive to
virtue; omphaloscopy for some reason is omitted. Teams
of such mental-moral athletes, living "the life of interest-
affection, a way of life which is a psychiatry, an economy,
and a policy," may perhaps promote a new mutation in
social evolution, even if no super-nova blows up in time
to help them out. At least we must try it; "our choice is
to go on to a new state of being, or end."

Thus the gospel according to Heard. It has its soft
spots; in dealing with the problem of evil he has to
come down to maintaining that outside of man, who
causes evil by believing that the individual is an end in
himself and not a phase of the Larger Life, there is
really not nearly so much evil as people think. But all
gospels have their soft spots, and this is no time to look
a gift gospel in the mouth—especially a psychiatric gospel offered to a neurotic age teetering on the verge of
lunacy. We have his word for it, however, that no morality is any good unless it is based on the latest cosmology;
so it seems necessary to take another look at his unbiased observation of reality, even at the risk of being set
down as what he calls a "rationalistic materialistic ethi-
cist." (Belloc has too much respect for the English
language to apply so barbarous an epithet even to the
foulest heretic.)

There is a good deal of scientific evidence which tends to discredit a purely mechanistic interpretation of the universe; there also remains a good deal of evidence on the other side. Of the evidence cited by Heard, how much is fact, how much plausible hypothesis, and how much cockeyed error, no man yet knows (except Heard). The one thing sure is that, like all scientific evidence, it consists of selections from the phenomena of the universe apprehended by the human senses and integrated by the human mind. Heard's criterion is simple; such selections as do not suit his scheme are dismissed as the offspring of greed and fear—or, like the evidence of astronomy, omitted altogether. Which is curious, since astronomy offers the most compelling proof, to the lay mind, of something in the universe that transcends mere mechanism.

Heard mentions astronomy only to remark that "the unexpected way in which our mathematical calculations tally with astronomical observations shows that our minds and the universe-mind think in the same manner." A little further consideration of astronomy (as distinguished from what some astronomical theorists have said on their day off) might be less encouraging. So far as astronomy can yet determine, the chief business of the universe seems to be quite alien to anything that is called life by residents of this planet. We may possibly be able to think like God, on an infinitesimal scale, but there is to date no more evidence in the stars than there is on earth that the emotions which we regard as the finest flower of human character are adumbrations of any attributes of Deity. Some faint perception of a Power in the universe, not ourselves, that does not give a damn for righteousness as we understand it—that is what you get, so far, from astronomy. The Voice from the whirlwind that told Job where to get off has yet to be effectively answered by Mr Gerald Heard.

Something seems to be wrong, then, with the either-or formula; materialism may be as completely exploded as he says it is, and still his engaging cosmology may not be quite exact. It is possible to argue, of course, that Man is to date the highest expression of the Force that is the universe; but the definition of "highest," in that case, is biased by local patriotism. Man can write a *Hamlet,* a Fifth Symphony, but he cannot yet bring forth Mazzaroth in his season, or guide Arcturus with his sons—achievements that may be rated more highly, by extra-terrestrial critics.

To be sure Mr Heard says that his cosmology and morality are only tentative, and most of his evidence is, at first, insinuated with weasel words; but as soon as he gets going his hypotheses become not only certainties but premises. Every "if" is a springboard from which he takes off gaily to another "if," till presently you discover that these tenuous possibilities have somehow become the solid granite blocks of a pyramid, on whose apex stands Mr Gerald Heard, triumphantly proclaiming, "Since we are now certain of the foregoing, it follows, etc."

For he atones for any carelessness about premises by sternly logical reasoning. "Must" is his favorite word, especially for people with whom he disagrees. If they believe such and such, they must come to the following conclusion; and accordingly they must behave thus and so, whether they do or not. This logic has some bearing on the accuracy of his picture of this mechanomorphic world, the City of Destruction from which we all must flee. It is a pretty bad place just now, God knows, but you can hardly put all the blame on Newton, Darwin, and Freud. Was it they who corrupted the devout Shintoists who are devastating China, the pious Catholics and Moslems who all but wrecked Spain? Nearer home, too, logic is a convenient substitute for observation. "If life has no meaning and must end with its extinction on this globe, it is not reasonable and purposive to work for such a goal." There are people who think it makes sense to try to behave decently, even if the dead rise not; but Mr Gerald Heard has never met them. "Even the noblest, without this assurance," must seek recreation and amusement where they can; "a few noble workers have actually taken to physical drugs," others dope themselves with domestic affection or a desire for fame.

Such anodynes are even worse, for home life means intensification of the individuality, ambition leads to arrogance—sins more heinous than adultery or embezzlement. There is no getting around it; people who refuse to accept the ethic deduced from the new cosmology go mad and beat their wives, plunge (after dreadful lives) razors and carving knives into their gizzards. This is so because it must be so.

You can prove anything by this sort of reasoning—criteria applied only to unfavorable evidence, the substitution of what logically ought to be for what is, calling a theory a theory when you introduce it and a fact as soon as you need it for a premise. Not the least of Heard's offenses is this: there is doubtless a good deal of truth, intermingled with error, in his cosmology, a good deal of sense mixed with nonsense in his ethic; but by his method it is utterly impossible to disentangle them. He darkens counsel by words without knowledge, and the hasty reader is likely to dismiss it all as hooey instead of trying to assay the percentage of precious metal in the ore.

And why waste space on such a book—especially when it is so badly written that only a dutiful reviewer is likely to read it through? Because it is a flagrant example of a type of thinking now common, and thoroughly pernicious—the either-or interpretation of history; pernicious because it encourages sloppy thinking, and because it is false. Belloc's book, far more respectable in style and content, falls into the same category of error; exclude all but two possibilities, set them down as inescapable alternatives, and you find that you have to overlook so protuberant a fact as Mussolini because he does not fit into your world-picture.

History seldom if ever runs in a channel with only two outlets. Napoleon Bonaparte, a man not unfamiliar with the forces that make history, once predicted that in fifty years Europe would be either Cossack or republican. Fifty years later republicanism was on the run, the Cossacks were barely holding their own, and Europe was dominated by Otto von Bismarck, a phenomenon not foreseen in Napoleon's either-or dichotomy. Abraham Lincoln, who possibly understood such matters better than Napoleon, once predicted that this government could not permanently endure half slave and half free; it must become either all slave or all free. Ask the share-croppers if he was right.

Yet we continue to hear from numerous thinkers that civilization faces a dilemma; and most of them (not Belloc, who knows what words mean) seem to think that one of its horns is well cushioned and comfortable, just what we need. Passing over this error in terminology, which threatens to become as universal as the misspelling of autarky, it might be remarked that civilization cannot possibly be facing all the dilemmas that are currently discerned—either Communism or Fascism;* either Catholicism or Communism; either this stream-lined Yoga by Heisenberg out of Blavatsky, or chaos. Something menacing and uncomfortable looms just ahead, which amateur zoölogists identify as one horn of a dilemma; more exact observation might classify the monster as a polylemma, a beast with seven heads and ten horns—and maybe some exits in between.

One of P. G. Wodehouse's philosophers in the bar-parlor of the Angler's Rest some time ago remarked that "Hitler stands at the crossroads—either he must shave it off or let it grow. There is no middle course." But Hitler and his facial adornment go serenely on, steering a middle course between the horns of the dilemma. Such navigation may be possible to larger and more valuable entities than Hitler's mustache.

---

* Do you remember (as the late Harvey Woodruff might have asked) way back when Communism and Fascism were supposed to be irreconcilably antipathetic?

Shaw and the Inner Light

SHAW AND THE INNER LIGHT

THE issuance of an omnibus containing most of the best of Shaw (whatever omissions individual readers may regret) in a good, legible type face is a rather startling reminder that a living author has become a classic of the past. As the Byzantines selected a few plays which in their perhaps fallible opinion were the best of Aeschylus and Sophocles, and those plays are all we know of Aeschylus and Sophocles today, so it is not wholly impossible that some day this selection might be all that is known of Shaw. Inevitably, then, the reader of plays and prefaces written between 1894 and 1924 finds himself wondering what it all amounts to now.

An attempt, however diffident, at a retrospective estimate of Shaw cannot be undertaken without filial piety by a member of the generation which in all English-speaking countries was formed chiefly by Shaw and Wells; nor indeed without a more disquieting emotion. We of that generation, who are still uncomfortably surprised when young men address us as Sir, were the first fruits of them that slept, the first graduating class of the

School of the Prophets; the first rude models, so far as education could form us, of the Samurai, the Supermen, the
new race which was to clean up the rubbish left around
by a still too anthropoid humanity. And as the world
of today is on the whole a worse place, and perceptibly
nearer the abyss, than the world of 1894, it might seem
a logical conclusion that something was fatally wrong,
either with us or with our teachers.

It was not so in 1913, and for what has happened since
1913 we sons of the prophets are not greatly responsible.
We did not make the war, nor are we the people who
will make the next one; Shaw has been popular in
Germany, but not with the military caste; and the people
whom he influenced in Japan do not govern Japan. In
England the Shaw-Wells influence was strongest and
the generation that came to maturity about 1913 was
most promising; but half the men of that generation are
dead, and the rest live only under reprieve. England
could be governed, indeed wholly populated, by Shav-
ians, and still be in danger of destruction in a Continen-
tal war begun by men to whom Shaw, if they had heard
of him at all, was only a misunderstood prophet of the
Superman. Granted that the seed sown by the prophets
sometimes produced a surprising crop, it was in the
main good seed; the trouble was that too often it fell
on stony ground. There are not yet enough of the children of light to dominate the policy of any great power,

let alone of the world; but that is no fault of the prophets.

Rereading this volume of Shaw after Wells's autobiography, I cannot see that they made any major mistake except underestimating the magnitude of the task that must be done before pre-history will have ended and history can begin. It grew while they were attempting it; the food of the gods produced giant rats, full-grown, before it brought any supermen to maturity; man's best achievements kept turning against him. Preventive medicine and humanitarian sentiment preserve millions whom hard-boiled Nature would sentence to an early death, salutary to the race; while the Wright brothers' triumph over Nature threatens to lead to the killing of millions who ought to live. Shaw and especially Wells foresaw a good deal of this, foresaw too what ought to be done; but their insight (like all other insight, to date) stopped short of devising the means of doing it.

Wells used to hope that some catastrophe might shock mankind into repentance; but we have had two catastrophes and those who flee from the City of Destruction are still few, nor are they agreed as to their destination. Shaw pooh-poohs the individual conversions of Salvationist Christianity; yet apparently he once hoped for a sort of mass conversion—that is, a great number of simultaneous individual conversions—under the pressure of common sense. We still wait for that glorious day; but the man who preached so powerfully against uprooting the wheat with the tares in heathen lands must realize that even in England a violent uprooting might do more harm than good. Once Shaw thought that abolition of property would be a cure-all; but more fundamental even than Communism in his creed is insistence on the freedom of the spirit. Russia of today may be more to his taste than England of the nineties, but one need not ask what would happen to a contemporary Russian who wrote about the society he lives in as Shaw writes about the society he lives in.

Wells once saw in Lenin's Communist Party the nearest approach to the "competent receiver" for a bankrupt world—a disciplined company purged of all selfish appetites but the lust for power and the pride of omniscience. These are considerable exceptions; a body with the same virtues and not dissimilar faults had been in existence for three hundred years before Lenin, and the Society of Jesus has not perceptibly improved the world except in the eyes of those who accept its premises. So in the Communists of 1934 Wells found a "trained obduracy to facts" that drove him to something as near despair as he can feel. Shaw came late to the quest for the competent receiver; in the preface to *Saint Joan* he dreamed of a Catholic Church catholic enough to include Protestants and heretics, a Church which would "inculcate and encourage free-thinking with a complete belief that thought, when really free, must by its own law take the path that leads to the Church's bosom." An engaging idea, but it involves a logical contradiction that was apparent to the Church a thousand years before Shaw was born; consequently there has never been such a Catholic Church, nor is it ever likely, even if you re-name it the Communist Party. You cannot combine dogma and evolution.

If in these matters the prophets went astray, nobody else has found the road they missed; and if more people are looking for it now than were looking for it forty years ago, the credit is largely due to Shaw and Wells. For all the differences between them (the chief one is Shaw's distrust of science) the substance of their mes-sages is identical. We must be about our Father's busi-ness, without letting ourselves be hampered by triviali-ties; that business is the establishment of the Kingdom of Heaven on earth; we must be born again before we can enter into the kingdom, but we shall know the truth and the truth shall make us free. Not a novel message; but that may only mean that certain truths are apparent to every mind which reaches a sufficient stature. Un-fortunately when truth frees the sort of human beings we have at present, the result is not always what the prophets hoped. Socrates, it has been observed, set men free and the immediate results were Alcibiades and

Critias; no wonder their fellow-citizens put their teacher to death. Give Shaw credit for realizing that the truth can be rightly used only by supermen, whom he would produce by education and eugenics.

Nobody can refute the eugenic side of his argument, for it has not seriously been tried. But Shaw's theory of education has been accurately summarized by Wells—"to let dear old Nature rip." This rests on the postulate that Nature is at bottom benevolent, as the Modernist clergy put it—or perhaps rather than at bottom, at the top. Man is part of Nature and the Life Force, pushing ever onward and upward, reaches its peak in Man's steadily improving best intention. But we are no longer so sure as we were thirty years ago that Nature (or God, if you prefer) regards Man as its highest product; nor are we so confident in the native goodness of Man. Goodness has to be thought out and worked for, against intra-human as well as extra-human obstacles. In the notes on *Caesar and Cleopatra* Shaw implies that the great man is one who does exactly what he wants; but that depends on what he wants. Caesar did what he wanted and so did Dillinger. Let Nature rip, and your supermen are likely to be Goerings or Huey Longs.

Even Shaw's triumphs have not always turned out as he hoped. There was no institution which he assailed more violently and assiduously than the Home. On the whole the Victorian home (though it had its merits, in its day) deserved his reproaches; and eventually before his trumpet blasts its walls came tumbling down. In Russia it collapsed most completely; and now the Russians seem to be discovering that if the Home does not exist, it is necessary to invent it. They have had a very Shavian marriage system—admirable in theory, calculated to preserve the freedom and self-respect of husband and wife; but unfortunately it turned out to be bad for the children, besides encouraging irresponsible libertines. The Shavian system had made no provision for irresponsible libertines; but once the food of the gods was on the market, anybody could grow fat on it.

Shaw contributed as much as any one man to the economic and political liberation of women, again with unforeseen consequences. He never knew much about women except in their epicene aspects; in *Man and Superman* he mistook accidental and temporary fruits of nineteenth-century English culture for the essential nature of the Eternal Feminine. Whether there is any such eternal and essential nature, God only knows; but at any rate women have not used the vote to impose a tax on bachelors, and if Mrs Warren's profession is no longer so flourishing, one reason is that there is so much amateur competition. Shaw might reply that the economic liberation is still incomplete; a woman who works every day to support herself cannot afford children. And it is true that women rich enough to have their doings chronicled on the society pages are much given to bearing children to successive husbands, as Shaw predicted; though the selection is not always as eugenic as he would have it. At any rate, economic and intellectual liberation has not yet got rid of irrational emotion; a woman may have the strongest theoretical objections to property rights in love, she may not need her man as a bread-winner, and still she can be miserable when she loses him. Shaw has seen what sexual emotion can do to people, but his writings about it suggest a learned treatise on alcohol-ism by a man who never was drunk. (Yes, even the letters to Ellen Terry; their violent protestations are pretty ob-viously the big talk of a man who knows what he ought to say and is confident that his bluff will never be called.)

These might seem considerable blemishes on a major prophet, but there is more than enough to offset them. If you believe at all in the long-term value of liberty, in the right to search for truth, you must honor a man who has done as much for it as anyone of our time. He broke up the arid crust of mental topsoil that hampered growth; if the humus beneath it was not as fertile as he had hoped, he can hardly be blamed. Get rid of the shams, the pretenses, the encrusted conventions that have outlived their utility, and get down to what is real; that was his message, and he shouted it with such fervor,

such insistence, and ultimately such success that it does
not greatly matter if he was wrong in a few details.
Reality was not always as workable a material as he expected; but it is the material we have got to learn to
work with, if we have any faith in human possibilities
at all.

"I do not see moral chaos and anarchy as the alternative to romantic convention," he wrote in 1898; "and I
am not going to pretend to merely to please the people
who are convinced that the world is held together only
by the force of unanimous, strenuous, eloquent, trumpet-
tongued lying." His opponents, not being all the conscious liars that he seemed to think, replied in kind; and
indeed there was some excuse for the reproach of in-
tentional paradox against a man who attacked property
and marriage from the economic bombproof built for
him by a rich wife, and abused capitalism, imperialism,
vaccination, and beefsteak with indiscriminate vehe-
mence. But when he insisted that he was merely one of
the rare people with "normal" vision he was nearer
right than his antagonists. His assertion that there had
been no noteworthy social and ethical progress since
Caesar's day sounded absurd in the nineteenth century,
but a third of the way through the twentieth we cannot
very confidently dispute it. The economics, the sociology,
the ethics of *Mrs Warren's Profession* are as sound today
as they were forty years ago; and a world that has seen

war will no longer question his picture of it in *Arms and the Man.*

For all his distrust of science and his retrospective admiration, in later years, for medieval Catholicism, Shaw is a quintessential product of the Renaissance and the Reformation. Fairly enough he criticizes Shakespeare's characters (and their creator) for having no social responsibility, no sense of being part of a social organism; which was a failing of the Renaissance. But we owe to the Renaissance and the Reformation the revival of the faith that this world is not necessarily a vale of tears, that perhaps something can be done about it; and that the way to do something about it is to let the individual follow his inner light as far as it may lead him. So far we have not done as much about it as had been hoped; individual endeavor has gone farthest in the economic field, where its successes eventually proved anti-social; and in the face of the obvious need for collective restrictions on the individual in that field, it is not surprising that a good many of the weaker brethren have become convinced that we cannot get along without collective control of everything, even thought.

Shaw always knew better. One of his most insistently repeated arguments for collective control of property is that only thus can you liberate the spirit and give it a chance to get somewhere. After Shaw's attack on romance read Cabell's defense of it, and you will see that the difference is the difference between a basic optimism and a basic pessimism about human potentiality. For all his surface hedonism and his irreverent treatment of hagiology, Cabell's spirit is that of the medieval Catholic; Shaw's is that of the Protestant whom nothing can silence but the stake. It seems more plausible now than it did forty years ago that the medievalists may have been right; perhaps God (or Nature, or the Life Force, if you prefer) has set insuperable limitations, internal and external, on human accomplishment. Nevertheless some men and some women are so made that they will go on trying till they drop in their tracks, and no man has ever set forth their creed more powerfully than Shaw.

"I sing the philosophic man," says Don Juan in the scene in hell; "him who seeks in contemplation to discover the inner will of the world, in invention to discover the means of fulfilling that will, and in action to do that will by the so-discovered means." How does he discover that inner will? Why, by convincing himself that his own inner will is the world's will despite any evidence to the contrary; he understands the tendency of evolution better than his persecutors. The classic instance in Shaw's works, of course, is Joan of Arc. Mencken, I believe, has remarked that the hero of the Eroica Symphony is not Napoleon but Beethoven; so the protagonist of *Saint Joan* is Bernard Shaw disguised as a peasant girl of medieval Lorraine. He has matured now; he is no longer so defiantly proud of his singular-ity, so sure that the opposition is a mere pack of leather-lunged liars; but he is as inflexible as ever. But a finer type than Joan, and one more relevant to this age of uncertainty, is Lavinia of *Androcles and the Lion*—not quite sure, at the end, for what she is dying, but sure that there is something worth dying for, even if you can find no better name for it than spiritual integrity. These are the true glory of Shaw's plays, these stubbornly undissuadable followers of the Inner Light. Even in so relatively light a work as *Fanny's First Play* there is a difference in kind between Mrs Knox and the rest of the conventional suburban parents. In their world the division is between the Respectable and the Disreputable, in her world it is between Right and Wrong; and she can recognize her daughter as one of her own kind, no matter how they may differ on the rightness of assaulting the police. For all Shaw's copious propaganda for collectivism, he is greatest and may be remembered longest as Mr Valiant-for-Truth, the individualist Protestant prophet, and saint. Sometimes he falls short of saintliness? So did all the saints, sometimes; but it was forgiven them, in consideration of their loyalty to their Voices, their Daimonion, their personal revelation.*

---

* This appreciation of the best of Shaw is not vitiated by recent exhibitions of the worst of Shaw—his comments on current affairs which, beginning apparently as a mere straining for

There remains Shaw the artist; but nothing that anybody can say about him can add to his stature. In a theater almost wholly given over, when he began, to physical or economic or emotional conflicts, he proved that the intellectual conflicts of characters of sufficient stature could be far more interesting than love-and-money problems, when handled by a dramatist of genius. Above all a comedian of genius; for tragedy deals with problems which are apt to become out of date, the peripeties of comedy have a more durable interest. Even the pilgrims of the inner light will be meaningless, if we fall back into a new medievalism. As Shaw himself wrote, "All the assertions get disproved sooner or later; and so we find the world full of a magnificent debris of artistic fossils, with the matter-of-fact credibility gone clean out of them, but the form still splendid." In comedy there is less assertion; but even comedy needs some intellectual content, and nobody else ever gave it so much as Shaw, unless perhaps Aristophanes.

Unfortunately Aristophanes devoted his genius to the upholding of a social and ideological system that was

---

paradox, proceeded in a descending spiral till they touched an all-time low in his remarks on the Russo-Finnish War. If what Shaw says about Finland is true then *Androcles* and *Saint Joan* are only lies that he told us, to bog us down still further in the morass of bourgeois sentimentality. It seems more probable that he was right the first time.

doomed to crack up no matter how hard he tried to save it; he would have had to be on the same side as Socrates to be as good as Shaw. Moreover, you can no longer understand much of what Aristophanes was talking about without a long classical training. Some of Shaw already begins to date; but not very much—at least in the perhaps ill-focussed eyes of one who as he rereads these plays cannot forget the impression they made on him at the first encounter.

Take, for instance, *Fanny's First Play,* which Shaw dismisses as a mere potboiler. Its only serious content, an attack on Respectability and the Home, may be sounding brass and tinkling cymbal to the young people of today, who cannot imagine a time when Respectability and the Home were important enough to be worth attacking. Yet they might enjoy it almost as much as their parents did. When I was young it seemed to me the funniest play I had ever seen; and it still seems so, after a subsequent experience including such diversely cerebral comedies as *Once in a Lifetime* and *Desire under the Elms.* Beside such comedy as Shaw wrote until the war threw the comic aspects of life into the background, all other comedy is as the crackling of thorns under a pot.

On the Eve: Reminiscences of 1913

ON THE EVE: REMINISCENCES OF 1913

IT was lately and casually remarked in public print that 1913 was the peak year of human felicity; to which opinion persons older than its author, and persons younger, have taken some exception. Everybody, they object, thinks that the peak of human felicity was the year in which he first began to sit up and take notice. Why should a man who happened to leave college in 1913 erect an accident of chronology into a philosophy of history, to the discredit of all the years in which other men left college and went out to see if the universe was as represented? . . . Well, I shall try to tell you.

Granted that I am prejudiced in favor of 1913 because it was the year in which I first came to the surface. Granted that the middle generation to which I now belong finds the Golden Age always in the past—the good old days when you could get a dinner with wine for what the hors-d'oeuvres cost now, when traffic and livers were less congested, and everything was veiled with a glamor which seems beyond recapture. Granted too that for the young, except in times of direst cataclysm, the Golden Age is always here and now, so that Ovid spoke for all the Younger Generations of all time when he wrote:

Prisca juvent alios, ego me nunc denique natum
Gratulor; haec aetas moribus apta meis.

Still, I think that we of 1913 found a better here and now than any generation which will follow us for some decades to come. Every younger generation is the heir of all the ages; but in our time the assets of the estate had accumulated to a legacy beyond all imagining, and we had not yet discovered that they were offset by some appalling liabilities. In other words, we came up before the war—just before the war—in what seems to the retrospective eye an age of incredible innocence and security.

II

Security. . . . For forty years in Europe, for fifty years in America, there had been no great war to check material and intellectual progress. Wars were still fought, but only in remote and romantic regions such as Manchuria, South Africa, the Balkans, Mexico; and only outlandish nations engaged in them on any considerable scale. Never since the Pax Romana had the Western world had so long a breathing spell, and never had it been so well equipped to take advantage of it. Wealth piled up at a rate undreamed of; there was more ease, more leisure for thought as well as recreation. Problems still existed, but it was generally agreed that human ingenuity and good will would solve them in the course of time.

Even in Europe, where I was living when the year began, the average man had never felt so secure. There was an increasing tension in international relations, diplomats exchanged politely menacing notes, general staffs laid plans for invasions, military budgets grew ever larger, there were recurrent crises. But of all this the average man knew only what he read in the papers; whereas he had daily first-hand knowledge of the growing internationalism of business, travel, sport, amusement that promised to make frontiers in Europe no more than lines on the map. There had been internationalism before, but it was limited to the Church, the nobility, the educated classes. This new internationalism touched, in the cities at least, everyone.

So war seemed an outgrown bogy-man of the childhood of the race. Was there a crisis? Well, there had been a crisis year before last and would be a crisis year after next; but the issue would be no more than a diplomatic triumph of one side or the other, the resignation of one Minister of Foreign Affairs, and the decoration of his rival. Mr Norman Angell had lately demonstrated that war was no longer profitable even to the victors; so if the danger ever became real the international bankers would prevent war. Or the international Socialists; or, if all else failed, the German Emperor, whose quarter-century of peaceful rule we were just then celebrating, would interpose his unanswerable veto.

So most of Europe felt, outside the governing circles. But how much more secure was America! Europe, to us, was the storied Old World, whose cathedrals and castles we viewed on summer tours but whose problems lay outside our sphere. We had problems of our own, about which the muckrakers had for some years been making a loud disturbance; but in 1912 we had gone to Armageddon, and most of us had come home fairly well satisfied with the result. The moderates had elected Wilson, the radicals had got rid of Taft, and the conservatives could thank God that at any rate they had beaten Roosevelt. Now the obviously needed reforms could be enacted, without much danger that reform would run wild.

True, 1913 was a year of business depression, as anyone who was then hunting his first job must remember. But the depression was easily explained. Republicans blamed it on a Democratic administration, Democrats laid it to the machinations of Republican wielders of the Money Power who wanted to discredit the administration. In any case, the business cycle was as much a part of the order of nature as seedtime and harvest. No one dreamed that perhaps our whole system had some incurable defect. There would be ups and downs in business as in international politics; but nothing really disastrous could ever happen again.

In this confidence we who came into our inheritance in 1913 could feel free to give our attention to the normal concerns of young people—love, amusement, and ideas. It seems to me that never since then has amusement had quite the tang or ideas quite the confident assurance; that even love has never since been quite so delicately flavored a blend of reality and illusion. . . . Laugh, if you like; but let me tell you.

III

Innocence and security. . . . But it did not seem innocent at the time; that was part of its charm. Our moral mentors told us that it was an age of unprecedented license and corruption, and that we boys and girls who had just cracked our shells were a brood of vipers from the pit. Why? Well, a fundamental change in manners, first visible two or three years earlier, was now in full swing; and behind it lay an almost equally fundamental change in ideas. The resultant product was what we then called, and not altogether unjustly, the emancipation of women. It was at last being admitted that women were people, even if all the implications of that concession were not yet apparent. The intellectual double standard had broken down, and the clergy correctly foresaw that the breakdown of the physical double standard would be an early consequence.

This is old stuff now, but it was new stuff then, and what has happened in subsequent decades of the new era was less decisive than what happened in the first two years. The change was the fruit of half a century's fermenting ideas; but what touched it off, about 1911, was the accidental coincidence of the revival of dancing and a wave of moral reform. Everybody was dancing now. The slashed skirts invented to make dancing easier had disclosed the long-guarded secret that ladies had legs; respectable women in increasing number had begun to smoke, and to drink in public places. Worst of all, it was now permissible for men and women, together, to talk about sex, provided it was treated on a high plane, as a social problem that could never have any personal application. (I would not say it never did have a personal application, but that happened more rarely than young people of today might believe.) But sex talk first came in by a side door.

Past centuries had accepted prostitution as a necessary evil. The nineteenth century still accepted it, on condition that it was never mentioned. But about 1910 there began a successful agitation for the abolition of the red-light districts of American cities; and to abolish them you had to mention them. Suddenly nice women discovered that what they had always known but had never dared to talk about could be discussed with propriety, provided you called it the white slave problem and insisted on the need of wiping out this blot on civilization. It was assumed in those days that every prostitute was an unwilling victim, a white slave, and that the lords of this nefarious traffic daily prowled the streets in search of new prey.

Hence the story of the young matron from Glen Ridge, or Garden City, or New Rochelle—everybody who told it knew somebody who knew her personally, and it was as much as your life was worth not to believe it—who came to town for a day's shopping and sat down in a subway car beside a man who stealthily pricked her with a poisoned needle; whereupon she lost consciousness and was carried off—over his shoulder, presumably—to a life of shame. Hence the frequent arrest of unfortunate males who had happened to sit down in subway cars beside women with hives and active imaginations. Hence a flood of plays about virtuous girls trapped by white slavers—plays that were denounced by the clergy, endorsed by forward-looking social workers, raided by the police, and fierily defended in magazine articles on "Public Conscience and the Stage."

Naïve? Childish? Unreal? Yes, as a childish un-
reality hangs over all the doings of the Golden Age.
But I think it was healthier than the bored indifference
with which the public, in the days of prosperity and
prohibition, regarded the doings of our racketeers; not
to mention the scandalous disclosures about the doings
of the New York vice squad and women's court some
years ago. The public conscience of 1913 may have
been adolescent and hysterical; still there was a public
conscience. We may have misconceived our problems
and have been largely mistaken in what we tried to do
about them; still, we felt that when there was a problem
something could be and ought to be done about it. Such
a public conscience, municipal and national, did not reappear for nearly two decades. New York is a far
more civilized city now than it was a few years ago; but
it needed the double impact of hard times and some
atrocious scandals to make us go back to the house-
cleaning job that John Purroy Mitchel began in 1913.

At any rate, the white slavery uproar gave the women
freedom of speech such as had not been known in centuries, just at the moment when they gained an unprecedented freedom of movement. Before 1911 Virtue had
been segregated almost as closely as Vice. Young men
might prowl about, but nice girls went out only under
chaperonage, to selected places; and the middle-aged of

both sexes resigned themselves to the somnolent fireside as a matter of course.

The new dances changed all that; anybody could dance them and everybody tried. Above all it was the age of dancing—and of rejuvenation. Father and mother, puffing away in the turkey trot, worked the fat off their bodies and their minds too; for the moment, all the world seemed young. The frontier of senescence had all at once been pushed back twenty years, so that we who were just beginning could count on a youth far longer than any generation before us had ever known.

IV

It ran all over the world, this dancing craze, the latest and most pervasive phase of the internationalism of culture and interest that had grown up in decades of peace. In London and Paris, Berlin and New York, the surface of society, the interests of the people one met, were the same; all the world over it was the age of tango teas. Not that many of us could dance the tango, though we all tried; nor did we drink much tea. In fact we did not drink much of anything; in a world so full of a number of things liquor was a subsidiary item; we used it as the spark, not as the fuel.

Smoking, for the girls, was a more important gesture. All young people want to kick up their heels and defy convention; most of them would prefer to do it at a not too heavy cost. As a play of Shaw's then current put it, they need to lose their respectability while retaining their self-respect. His heroine did that by going to jail for beating up on a cop, but for most girls of the day smoking met the need. It had till lately been a badge of infamy, it still aroused the fury of conservatives; yet no sensible person could believe it did any real harm. As a safety valve, the girls have never had anything like it.

But it was not only what the girls did that excited the conservatives, but where they did it. Now that Vice had been driven out of the restricted district and Virtue had been lured away from the fireside, institutions sprang up—mostly around Times Square—for the entertainment of both. We called them cabarets; they were much like the modern night club except that they were day clubs too, doing their biggest business at the tango tea. Before about 1912 it was generally true that the righteous could be seen in certain places, the wicked in certain others; now the two streams intermingled for the first time. . . . So nice girls went to tango teas at cabarets, and drank cocktails, and smoked cigarettes, and talked sex with boys; and of course there was a tremendous uproar.

The clergy trumpeted denunciations, and lay conservatives joined in. Indignant Senior takes his pen in hand to write to the *Times:* "Who is at home now?

All are hasting and chasing after the Great God Amusement." So Indignant Senior was writing in Babylon,
when he had to chop his complaint in a brick. A bishop,
rarely liberal, advises his clergy to stop denouncing the
slit skirt—which was going out of style anyway—and
instead preach Jesus Christ and Him crucified; with the
approving echo of an editorial writer who observes that
holy men need not dwell in detail on unholy things, since
"women who listen to sound religious and ethical teaching will not dress immodestly." The police order all
cafés but John Dunston's to close at one A. M., Mayor
Gaynor denouncing them as "places of all-night orgies,
drunkenness, and shamelessness." Thomas Healy, lock-
ing his bar at the appointed hour, advises his guests that
the law permits them to stay and finish their food;
whereupon the police swarm in and throw the diners out
by force. (As it happened, in their enthusiasm they also
threw out the District Attorney, so that crusade was
promptly stepped on.)

This Thomas Healy was renowned for his exorbitance;
he charged a quarter for a cocktail or highball which
at any other cabaret cost fifteen cents. But even Healy
had never heard of the cover charge. It was, you perceive, a simple age; when the Stock Exchange table took
up half a column in the newspaper, and a dinner with
wine could be had for half a dollar. Not the best wine,
or the best dinner, but good enough for youth. And

orchestra seats at the theater were two dollars apiece; and after the theater you could take your girl to a cabaret, and dance and drink till closing time for two or three dollars more. . . .

But it was not mere cheapness that gave a tang to amusement; it was our conscious defiance of conventions we did not respect. There were conventions which most of us did respect, but they were not yet in question. (For a minor instance, you could take your girl to Maxim's or Bustanoby's; you might perhaps take your wife to Joel Rinaldo's, but never your fiancée.) We leaped defiantly over the molehills our elders had made into mountains; having thus proved our strength and spirit we felt no need to explore the real mountains that loomed ominous a little farther on. They called us vile and abandoned, but we knew we were nothing of the sort; we had merely looked over the conventions of the day and rejected those which seemed superannuated. From the purely hedonistic standpoint, I think we got more fun out of life than the young people of a later age when no conventions were any more than what Mr Cabell calls "inefficient and outmoded monsters in the way."

V

We had ideas. Bernard Shaw had provided most of them, but a score of English writers were following the

trail he blazed. It was in England, I think, that the
pre-war generation was most promising—boys and girls
who were keen and zestful, at once polished and enthusiastic. (Those lightfoot lads are dead now, or dis-
heartened; and the rose-lipped girls grow old without
husbands.) American writers still lagged behind. The
big problem novel of 1913 was Mr Winston Churchill's
The Inside of the Cup, dealing with the agitations of an
Episcopal clergyman who was not sure his church was
right about divorce; and Mr Henry Sydnor Harrison was
the rising hope of American letters. Poetry made a better
showing; a year or so before, it had broken out like a
rash all over the corn belt, and now a poet sat on every
fence post, caroling free verse. Pretty good verse, too;
those blended carolings seemed only the prelude to a
great national festival of song—but the prelude turned
out to be all of the show. Where are those poets now?
Some of them write good biographies of Lincoln and
some write bad biographies of Lincoln; some of them
write indifferent fiction, and the most have merely folded
up in silence.

But though we still had to import most of our ideas,
we had them; and each of us believed that his own
idea would presently bring into being the all-but-perfect
society. The march of civilization had freed man from
his traditional worries—food and security. Ruinous wars,
destructive social upheavals were as certainly outgrown

as famine, pandemic diseases, religious bigotry. Man was free to think; he could think boldly, for the machinery of society was foolproof. If society still needed improvement, that could be accomplished by the direct primary, or the popular election of senators, or the initiative, referendum, and recall; or by giving the vote to women.

More and more woman suffrage became the most discussed of issues; but it was only an aspect of the profounder issue of feminism—perhaps the most widespread and certainly the most exciting of the millennial hopes of the time. Women wanted to be people—to step down from their Victorian pedestals and associate with men on the same level. We young men wanted no Victorian slave-goddesses, but comrades and companions, free and equal, who would be intelligently interested in our interests; and who of course would also feel for us, and inspire in us, that mysterious emotional intoxication that the nineteenth century called romantic love.

Well, the ladies came down—farther down, perhaps, than they expected, but few people would doubt that the world is on the whole a good deal better off. But you can't have everything, and we pre-war feminists expected it; most of us would have been shocked if we had foreseen that fifteen years later André Maurois would describe modern love as a sort of sensual friendship. We wanted friendship and we wanted sensuality; but we also wanted and expected more—more, perhaps, than there is.

But in 1913 we did not know it was more than there is. We wanted and got girls who were friends and comrades; but they had not yet left off being a little remote and mysterious. Physically, they were swathed from neck to instep, as women always had been; even when they bathed in the surf they wore knee-length skirts, and stockings. But their clothes looked all right at the time, as whatever girls are wearing at any time looks all right to boys of their own age. Chubbiness, in those days, was the feminine ideal; the boyish form was still unknown, and Bonwit Teller's advertisements pictured corsets for the normal woman such as Bonwit Teller still may sell, but only Lane Bryant would dare to advertise.

But these were mysteries, at least in theory, to the young men of 1913; and in such matters theory counts for more than practice. Mentally, too, the girl of 1913, emancipated though she tried to be, had her reticences which would have seemed stuffily prudish a little later, after we had heard of Freud. We stood just on the threshold of revelation, and had not learned that here too we expected more, perhaps, than there is. . . .

Yes, love in those days was a delicately flavored blend of reality and illusion, of candor and mystery.

You took a girl to a tango tea; she drank with you and smoked with you, like a man and a brother. As a person, a free and equal comrade, intelligently interested in the world you and she were going to live in, she talked to you—about everything. "Everything" generally meant sex; it startled you to realize that this creature whom your early training and the books you had read had taught you to consider as something strange, mysterious, and apart was a human being like yourself, with a body and a mind—two attributes which nineteenth-century doctrine had generally denied her. But just as you felt that this matter-of-fact impersonal discussion might be dimming an ancient glamor she did something, or said something, or looked something that made you realize that after all she was a creature of another and an incalculable sort. She was at once the seeker and the sought, a comrade and a mystery.

So we played our romantic comedy, and never dreamed that other actors, with other lines to speak, were about to burst in from the wings.

VI

Well, there is no use now in crying over spilt milk; especially as there was never so much milk in the pitcher as we thought. Our aspirations were fantastic and our doings absurd, considering the tremendous irony of what was coming; we look back at our unsuspecting selves as a Greek audience must have looked at the pride of unsuspecting Oedipus. What we did and what we hoped for alike seem naïve, childish, unreal.

Any tendency to humility that we of 1913 may possess has been abetted by our juniors. They tell us, truly, that we were a foolish and visionary lot, misled by all sorts of illusions. I understand that all that has been changed. "Post-war minds," writes the possessor of one of those minds in the *Outlook*, "have been disciplined and disillusioned." To the middle-aged observer the disillusion is more apparent than the discipline—except in the case of those unfortunates who, to buy release from the painful necessity of thinking, have sold their souls to the Party Line. Even the disillusion is selective; the post-war mind sees through the illusions of 1913, but I am not so confident as some of its possessors that it has attained to intuitive perception of eternal truth. But that may be just as well. Illusion is the most powerful of motive forces. Even our illusions of 1913 might have carried us a long way, though probably not where we expected.

Like all younger generations, we knew a great many things that are not so; but we meant well. I am old-fashioned enough to believe that, other things being equal, good intentions are more useful than bad intentions, or no intentions at all; but we, the last generation for some decades to live in a world of innocence and security, shall probably also remain for some decades the last that could have much faith in good intentions as such. The lesson of August 1914 was reënforced in October 1929; we live in a world of peril and uncertainty, paved with the good intentions of our ancestors—paving stones which have too often turned into stumbling blocks.

With an irrational optimism befitting an alumnus of the absurd age in which I came to the surface, I still believe that higher peaks of human felicity may be ahead; that our race, if it keeps on trying, might make a quite habitable place of the planet on which it resides. But it will be some time before anybody can expect the millennial dawn as confidently as young people expected it in the age of tango teas.

Purest of Pleasures

PUREST OF PLEASURES

IT seems to be widely felt that in times like these it is ignoble to seek pleasure, or even relaxation; the conscientious citizen of the world ought to be busy every moment trying to help correct the sad state of affairs in general, and has no right to slink back to self-indulgence in his ivory tower. Nobody who has friends in Europe can very seriously dispute that, as a general proposition; when he thinks of the misfortunes that have befallen better men, which he himself has escaped by a mere accident of geography, he cannot help feeling that he ought to be trying to do something about it—even if it appears that there is nothing in particular that he can do at the moment except to contribute to relief funds. Nevertheless any expert on industrial fatigue will tell you that you will probably do a better job, whatever your job may be, if now and then you stop thinking about it for a little while; and it would seem an excess of Puritanism to abjure this needed diversion just because you might incidentally find some pleasure in it.

The following remarks are an advertisement for the
people who find it at what is inaccurately termed the
bridge table. (Contract dummy whist is not "contract
bridge" any more than a man is the descendant of his
great-uncle; but it seems useless to combat an error so
long established.) Like miniature golf and mah jongg
in their several days, contract is a big business as well as
a sport; and a person engaged in the literature industry
must feel a certain shame when he reflects that about
the only branch of that industry which in the depth of
the hard times enjoyed any prosperity is the literature
of bridge. One bridge book sold two hundred thousand
copies in eighteen months, and I suspect that among its
half dozen closest competitors would be two or three
other bridge books. "Who gets the girl?" used to be
the ever-dependable theme of salable writing; but in
contemporary fiction almost anybody can get the girl,
so perhaps it is not surprising that this once popular
question has been supplanted by "Who gets the bid,
and what does he do with it?"

All of this has been a godsend to the bookstores, and
of course to the bridge experts as well. Their books sell
when other books die unwanted on the counters; they
syndicate daily bits of wisdom to newspaper readers all
over the country; they teach bridge, and in a thousand
towns over the country "pupil of Culbertson" gives the
degree of prestige that "pupil of Leschetizky" did in
days gone by.

But while, no doubt, the experts all like bridge, and would play it for fun even if they never made any money out of it, it must bring them harassment as well as pleasure; like any other big business men, they have their hours of worry about trade conditions, and when things are going well they wonder how long this will last. I am an average player (at least I hope so; some of my partners might challenge that claim), and what is here said applies to average players—not to the experts or to the enthusiastic incompetents who are as much of an obstruction to the game as is a hay wagon to boulevard traffic. In our own estimation, we average players are the salt of the earth; for we play the game well enough to have some understanding of it and some pride in it, and still not so well that our love of the pastime can ever be contaminated by any sordid hope of gain.

And there are a lot of us; if contract is not the national game, it is second only to golf, and certain tendencies of the times seem likely to make golf less popular from now on. In the larger cities it is a costly game; you must belong to a country club, and in the days of wholesale resignations from country clubs people who had not resigned found that their membership cost about as much to support as a margin in stocks. A good many people took up golf in the boom days because it had a snob value—to play it made you look like a member of the upper classes. But as the depression deepened, the upper classes came to look more and more like the lower classes; even if a man were prosperous he was afraid to show it because everybody he met would try to borrow money. So the snob appeal lost its value.

Also, golf seems to attract persons of a perverse and gloomy nature; some of my friends go out to play it in the same spirit of self-abasement that drove their medieval ancestors to lash themselves with knotted whips. But a man who wants to discourage himself nowadays can do it at far less expense by reading the morning paper.

None of these objections applies to contract. It requires no costly equipment; you do not have to go out in the country to play it; you are playing against other people, not against some theoretical standard of perfection, so if you stay in your own class you will suffer no more than an occasional moderate and salutary humiliation. This, I am convinced, is the first and great commandment for those who want to enjoy contract—stay in your own class. It will spare you mental anguish and it will save you money.

To say that you cannot enjoy a bridge game unless there is money on it is about as reasonable as saying that you cannot get interested in a woman unless she has a husband who might shoot you. If you really want the woman you will need no such irrelevant and supererogatory stimulation; and if you really like the game you will play it as well as you can, whether there is any money

up or not. Contract without a stake can be just as good
as if you were playing for a dollar a point. However,
there are people who feel otherwise—so many of them
that if you refuse to play for money you will be considerably restricted in your opportunities to play at all. But
stay in your own class and you will find that—since
the law of averages can be counted on to give you a fairly
even break in the cards from one year's end to another—
your game will just about pay its way.

Contract has further attractions for the reflective.
Plato held that smell was the purest of the sensual
pleasures because it involved no appeasement of pre-
existent pain. The joys of the table derive some of their
keenness from the preceding pangs of hunger; but no
man ever feels himself starving for agreeable odors.
"The pleasures of smell spring up suddenly and present
themselves in full force to a man who was not previously
conscious of any suffering; and when they have vanished
they leave no pain behind." Accordingly they are a hundred per cent net profit, and so are the pleasures of contract. The bridge player does not say, "When shall I
awake? I will seek it yet again." He may be keenly
aware of his lack of love or lack of money, but he does
not grow jittery because there is no card game going on.
He gives himself over to other preoccupations; and
when somebody whispers to him, "Will you make a
fourth?" the pleasures of the card table spring up sud-

denly and present themselves in full force to a man who was not previously conscious of any suffering.

Another merit of the game: as Lord Melbourne might have said, there is no damned nonsense of utility about it. You cannot pretend that it is a form of Service; golfers who are too puritanical to admit that they play golf because they like it will discourse at length upon its hygienic, cultural, and social benefits; but dealing the cards is no great exercise, and the bridge table is no place to meet your customers and talk business while you play. (Unless, of course, you enjoy conversational bridge; in which case you had better stop reading this article, and may consider yourself conspued by its author.) There is no good excuse for playing contract except the pleasure you get out of it.

Some attempt has been made to give the game an intellectual snob value; Mr Culbertson's *Bridge World*, for instance, bursts into the following rhapsody: "If bridge makes strange bedfellows, it is because the pleasures of the intellect are considered superior. Our common meeting ground is the play of intellect in its purest symbolic form." But this is hooey, and a man so shrewd as Culbertson must know it. To him and experts of his class the game does indeed present recondite mathematical-metaphysical beauties for the contemplation of the pure intellect; but these are as far beyond the grasp of the average player as are the high joys of Jeans or Ein-

stein. To play good bridge calls for intellect, but a specialized type of intellect adapted to playing bridge; it is
no more a sign of the general brain power flatteringly
imputed by the above quotation than is skill at chess.
Napoleon was a notably bad chess player; which is a
reflection on chess, not a reflection on Napoleon. If
bridge brains were good for anything but bridge, you
might expect this nation to be ruled by its tournament
stars; but except for Mr Vanderbilt, who sails yachts, I
cannot recall that any of them has been conspicously
successful at anything but bridge.

Another expert, Mr Shepard Barclay, is less flattering
to his public but more encouraging: "Bridge is not half
so hard to learn as some people fear." Maybe not, but
it is a good deal harder to learn than some other people
realize. The experts, no doubt, would like to have it
both ways: to play well is a proof of intellectual power,
yet anybody who buys the right book and applies himself
to the right system can learn to play well—a new mode
of purveying exclusiveness to the masses. It is true that
you cannot play good bridge without a bridge education
any more than you can practice good law without a legal
education; but mere reading of books and attendance at
lectures can no more make a firstrate bridge player than
it can make an Untermyer or a Darrow. I believe that
anybody of moderate intelligence can by diligent application become a sound bidder; but unless some card

sense is born in you, you will never be a really good player, even after twenty-five years of practice. *Crede experto.*

II

The mere existence of contract, and of its predecessors bridge and auction, is proof of this. They are all variants of whist, and they successively supplanted it in favor because they are easier than whist. Any good whist player will be a good contract player when he has mastered the elements of bidding; but millions of people who pass as good contract players because they bid their hands well and play them well (after the bidding has located most of the key cards) would be quite beyond their depth at whist, where the trump depends on chance and the location of the cards has to be inferred from the play.

Whist was so popular in the eighteenth century that (as the learned R. F. Foster records) at Florence whist tables were put in the opera-house boxes, and the music was valued chiefly as "increasing the joy of good fortune, and soothing the affliction of bad." But a game that makes such rigorous demands on the intelligence—or on the card sense, if you prefer—was soon undergoing modifications to make it easier for the average player; at least one of these, Boston, seems to have sprung up no more than twenty-five years after whist had become standardized. In Boston the essential principle of auction was already present; it is a little hard to understand why bridge, with its regression to a very elementary form of bidding, should have intervened. If bridge is really of Russian origin (I believe the Greeks also have a claim on it) its vogue is still less explicable; the game of vint, mentioned in Russian novels long before bridge was played in the West, is considerably more advanced; essentially it is auction without a dummy, and its scoring is in some respects an anticipation of contract.

However, bridge swept the world around the turn of the century, while vint never got outside of Russia; and millions of persons who had been dubbing along at whist found the new game easier and consequently more attractive. It gave an opportunity to cash in on your good hands (when you were the dealer) and escape without loss on your bad hands by bidding the low spade which in those days was never played. Your opponents could do the same, of course; there was more purpose in it than in whist, less chance and less demand on the intelligence. The addition of the "royal spade" bid rid the game of its one obvious weakness—and then, all at once, it was supplanted by auction.

Mr Foster, that inexhaustible fount of card history, says that auction was invented about 1903 by three members of the Indian civil service at a lonely hill station (readers of Kipling will infer that their fourth had been carried off by cholera) who thought of it only as a three-handed game. But the auction principle had long been familiar in Boston and Five Hundred; maybe one of the three recalled these pastimes, or maybe they learned vint from a Russian spy who had come down over the Pamirs. At any rate, when their three-handed game was played by four hands it was so much of an improvement over bridge that it needed only to be heard of to be adopted everywhere. And then, a few years later, came contract; which is to auction as Clos de Vougeot to home-made wine.

As a purely intellectual exercise the play in contract is far inferior to that in whist; you know too much before the first card is led. But the bidding imports an intellectual exercise of quite another order which is almost as good a discipline in applied psychology as poker. If contract has surpassed the vogue of auction, bringing new recruits to the card table and rekindling the enthusiasm of some of us who had begun to find auction something of a bore, it is because it is a better game, with far more action and far more suspense. In auction a good hand is irresistible; in contract it may be only an enticement to disaster unless you bid it right. No doubt the mere change in scoring has impressed some people with the conviction that contract is more of a game. Writing before the present contract scoring had alto-

gether supplanted the auction values, Foster observed
that the stake per point was reduced as the score was in-
creased; "why it would not be just as simple to advance
the stakes and keep to the already well-established values
is not explained." Here speaks the austere aristocrat;
the more practical Barclay provides the explanation.
"The higher score appeals to the childish attribute that
remains with all adults who are wise enough to avoid
growing up completely." However wise such avoidance
may be, plenty of adults have managed it with great
success; they feel that they are in fast company when
they play a game at which you can go down a couple of
thousand points on a single hand.

Perhaps contract has certain other advantages peculiarly adapted to these times. Its values, and its interest,
are detached, abstracted from reality, from all the
heterogeneous and too often unpleasant phenomena of
everyday living. I know of no mental exercise which
gives so complete an escape from the things you want to
escape from. Yet some of its principles have a timely application; in auction you might bid a little and win a
great deal, as you could in the empire-building America
of the nineteenth century; but in contract you must bid
and work for everything you get and risk a disastrous
penalty for miscalculation, as entrepreneurs are likely to
do in the frontierless and more static America of the future. Vulnerability—the principle that the higher you

have risen the more a mistake will cost you—is a concept easily grasped by the American public, which has so often seen the career of a distinguished man ruined by a private peccadillo which would be overlooked in a person of less prominence. (It could be wished that more of our distinguished men might be ruined by their public peccadillos, by their behavior in office.) And finally in an age of confusion and multiplicity, of an all too visible increase in what the physicists call the random element in the universe, there is a nostalgic charm about a game in which for a little while you devote yourself to a fixed and precise objective.

But all this may be fanciful. The great indubitable reason for the popularity of contract is its merit; more than any other card game it approaches the ideal balance between chance and skill. And the secondary and corollary reason is that more talent has been devoted to exploiting it professionally than was ever before expended on any card game. In which connection it is impossible to withhold the blue ribbon from Mr Ely Culbertson.

III

Rival experts may have had good reasons for disliking Culbertson, but they are all in debt to him, as every manager of a fight club anywhere is in debt to the late Tex Rickard; Culbertson's genius for ballyhoo did more than anything else to make contract a major sport and a big business. In the Culbertson odyssey fact and legend may be intertwined, but the story that he once taught psychology seems plausible enough; for he has practiced it with a brilliance hardly surpassed by Calvin Coolidge or E. L. Bernays. This talent would have made him successful in almost any line of business; that the accident of his marrying a bridge teacher made him apply his gifts to bridge was undoubtedly a piece of luck for the industry.

His competitors might not agree with that; but Culbertson's unpopularity in the trade is part of his showmanship. A man who frankly admits that he is the greatest egotist on earth and then goes on flaunting his ego in the face of his rivals and the public knows exactly what he is doing and why. Jack Dempsey, good-humored and likable in private, built up a public personality that roused the hatred of the crowd, and it made him a rich man; people who knew only his fighting face and his professional manner cheerfully paid fifty dollars in the tenuous hope of seeing him flattened out by a Frenchman or an Argentino. Culbertson modest and self-effacing would be only one of the crowd; Culbertson challenging and blatant infuriates his rivals; they trumpet their demand that Culbertson be abolished—and the public sees that it is the pack against Culbertson and concludes that this one man is the equal of them all.

And if there are plain citizens—not competing experts—whom Culbertson infuriates, why, that is more meat for Culbertson; he gets their money too. The latest list of his publications includes five of his own books, one by his wife, and three by other writers explaining the Culbertson system for players good, bad, or indifferent; along with two other books which seem, from the advertiser's description, to be derisive spoofs on Culbertson and all his works. Whether you like him or hate him, he will sell you a book to suit your taste. Such a combination of high impartiality and a nose for profit can hardly be found elsewhere; it is as if the works of Karl Marx were published, in the hope of gain, by the Republican National Committee.

Other bridge writers, plain blunt men, say what they have to say in plain blunt words; but Culbertson goes into flights of metaphor—the submerged reefs of distribution, the protection of the trump fortress, war tactics in open and mountainous country, etc. This may be quite genuine, the way the game appears to Culbertson's restless mind; at any rate it is good business. Read the other experts and you read about a game of cards; read Culbertson and you feel that you are involved in an enterprise of major importance. Even the famous and ridiculous one-hundred-and-fifty-rubber duel with Lenz was good publicity. "Let them hate me," said Domitian, "so long as they fear me"—which any modern publicity expert would amend to "Let them laugh at me so long as they talk about me." The astounding blunders in play which distinguished the first night of that contest may have been due to the well-advertised plethora of champagne; but bad play continued on later and presumably drier evenings, and I suspect that some of it was deliberate—a studied encouragement of the ordinary dub player, who will feel better when he sees those great geniuses Lenz and Culbertson gumming up good hands, even as you and I.

Praise of Culbertson's unique gift for publicity implies no lack of respect for the solider if less showy merits of his rivals. For some of their systems I have little use; but I surmise that if the leaders of politics and industry had bestowed on their trade, in the past twenty years, the amount of serious study and tolerably disinterested thinking that has been invested in bridge by the leaders of the bridge business, this country might be somewhat better off.

IV

But room must be made for the objections of the *advocatus diaboli*. Some of the people who do not like bridge dislike it with a quite inexplicable frenzy. They will tell you that it saps the brain power, if any, of the individual, and disrupts the household by its contentions; it sows discord between wife and husband, between friend and friend; it is nothing less than the terminator of delights and the separator of companions.

Well, most of the complaints about bridge boil down to this, that it is sometimes played by the wrong people. Too much liquor brings out your true nature, whatever that may be; and so does a bad bid, a disastrous takeout, a stupid play by your partner. People who crack under such a strain would crack under whatever strain might be imposed upon them, and I do not see that bridge can be blamed for it. The persons who feel it necessary to conclude each hand with a magisterial correction of their partners (and perhaps their opponents as well) have no place at the bridge table, or anywhere else where they might come into contact with civilized beings; and I do not know that they are more frequently found or more offensively conspicuous at the card table than in some other departments of life.

"Never reproach your partner," says Culbertson, "if there be the slightest thing for which you can reproach yourself." (On the other hand, do not reproach yourself if you think it would give undue encouragement to your partner's baser instincts.) This is not only Christian charity but good sense; the *practical* attitude toward your partner, Culbertson pursues, should be that of a "philosophical, sincere, and sympathetic friend." You share each other's joys, each other's burdens bear; and often for each other flows the sympathizing tear. "Partner, however weak, must feel that you sincerely respect his intelligence and efforts." And if this is odious pretense, if he is so weak that nobody could sincerely respect him—why, that is your fault for not choosing your company. First and foremost, stay in your own class.

You can't always do that when you go out for a social evening and find yourself in an unforeseen bridge game? No; but there is no law requiring a man who can play bridge to play it whenever he is invited. If you play with people you never met before you cannot complain when your partner continually talks over her shoulder to people across the room about her latest round-the-world cruise, meanwhile missing a couple of finesses and over-looking a discard or two. Of course, if you tell the hostess you don't play, and some other guest pipes up with "But you do; I've played with you!"—why, then you are trapped, and may as well resign yourself to whatever fortune fate sends you. But that is no peculiar fault of bridge; it may happen just as well to a man who pretends he doesn't dance because he is alarmed by the weight of his prospective partners. Social life can be made tolerable only by taking a firm stand on such matters; and if indignant hostesses resolve that they will never invite you again, you can always stay at home and read a book.

As for domestic discord, bridge never broke up a home that was not ripe for disruption anyway. If your wife is a very much better player than you, or a very much worse player, you had better not play with her; but you had better not play with anybody else who is very much better or very much worse. In the famous case of the Kansas City woman who shot her husband for failing to make his contract of four spades, the news reports omitted the essential points—what cards deceased had held and how he played them. But I suspect that if cards had never been invented she would have shot him over something else. Playing against a married couple I knew but slightly, I was shocked by their recriminations; and when I was dummy I suggested to the proprietor of the restaurant where we were playing that maybe the game had better be broken off before shots were fired. "Oh, that don't mean nothing with them two," he assured me. "They love each other like you don't see it any more." Evidently their emotional margin was so wide that they could do without philosophical and sympathetic friendship.

As to the vexed question of bisexual bridge in general, I think that men who say they don't like to play with women are putting the argument on a wrong basis. The point is that you get full value out of a bridge game only when it is a bridge game and nothing else; to play it well requires concentration, and if you are not going to try to play it well there is no point in playing at all.

It is probably true that women, more often than men,

regard a game of bridge as only an excuse for conversation—including some women who can play an excellent game when they choose to concentrate on it. But once again, pick your company and you will have no complaint; there are plenty of women who at the bridge table are willing to confine themselves to playing bridge, and would rather indulge in conversation over a few drinks. Call it the inveterate prejudice of a pre-war feminist, if you like, but I have little patience with the men who complain that "women" do this and that. Even Foster falls into this; "women," he says, "are great offenders in trifling matters, such as asking the dealer if she passed it, when nothing has been said; looking over the adversaries' hands as dummy, and then pushing dummy's cards forward as if arranging them, but in reality indicating which one to play. . . . There may be some remedy for this sort of thing, but so far no one seems to have found it."

Well, there is one unfailing remedy—do not play with women like that. You can find plenty of others—women who are good players and good sportsmen too.

V

There remain to be answered the weighty criticisms of a couple of psychologists, who burst into print during the Lenz-Culbertson duel. "Bridge may develop brains," said Professor Charles Gray Shaw of New York University, "but the quality of the brains developed is not worth cultivating." Still harsher was Professor Harold Swenson of the University of Chicago: "You couldn't drag a real thinker to the bridge table with a team of horses."

If this means anything except that a couple of professors were picking up crumbs of publicity from the mighty banquet of Culbertson, it means that Professor Swenson's definition of a real thinker is a man who couldn't be dragged to the bridge table by a team of horses. By any other definition he is demonstrably wrong. As for Professor Shaw, he is right this far—that the brains specifically developed by bridge are good for nothing much but bridge; but not so much can be said for his further statement that "the habitual bridge player lacks adequate emotional power and must play to stimulate his nerves."

If this, in turn, means that bridge is the refuge of men who do not like or are not pleasing to women, and women who do not like or are not pleasing to men, the only answer it calls for is a derisive snort. Confessing that I personally am one who prefers *Götterdämmerung* to *Tristan,* I could cite some of the best bridge players I ever met, of both sexes, who have plenty of emotional power and do not go to the card table when they want their nerves stimulated. Possibly Professor Shaw's intention was more general; in which case his remarks may be true of some bridge players. Some years ago I was in one of the minor European monarchies; and the day I left the capital a local newspaperman said to me, "Can't you stay over till tomorrow? We have a date to go up to the Palace and play bridge with the King." Somewhat flustered, I said that I could not aspire to such an honor. "Oh, it's no particular honor," he told me. "He gets lonesome up there at the Palace; the Dictator won't let him do any work, and he's always glad when somebody will come up to play bridge with him."

Bridge may be a needed stimulus to the nerves of unemployed royalty; but for us ordinary players its stimulation is intellectual, not emotional, even if the intellect it stimulates is of a specialized and unprofitable type. A philosopher, says Aldous Huxley, is a man who dreams of fewer things than there are in heaven and earth; and it is evident that Professor Shaw has never perceived the real attractions of bridge. Choose your company—people who play not much better than you do and not much worse, people who sit down at the bridge table to play bridge, not to talk about irrelevancies—and you will find yourself transported into another world. The agitations and exacerbations of everyday life drop away from you; for a while you dwell in a remote and austere realm of the pure intellect, uncontaminated by any practical applications; and as your game improves you may catch glimpses of some of those mathematical beauties of sequence, distribution, and arrangement such as perhaps the Absolute perceives when it contemplates Itself.

On the Gentility of Gentiles

ON THE GENTILITY OF GENTILES

EACH spring there arises in my family the problem of where we are to spend the summer; and among the countless summer colonies within two or three hours of New York whose prices are within the reach of a middle-class professional man the choice somehow narrows down in the end to the three or four settlements where we have spent previous summers. They offer plenty of variety; some are in the mountains, some beside the sea; some are addicted to golf, some to tennis; at one or two you have to do a good deal of dressing up, at the others you can wear anything you like; here the nucleus of New Yorkers is diluted by Brooklynites, there by Bostonians or Philadelphians. But in one respect all these resorts are alike; wherever we go, wherever we can afford to go, we can't ask the Rosenblatts down for a week-end.

Nor the Ecksteins, nor the Blaufarbs. The Ecksteins and the Blaufarbs would feel that they were slumming if they visited any of the summer colonies I could afford; at their country places they have Gentile neighbors,

Gentile friends—Gentiles who are rich enough and prominent enough to be able to afford to associate with anybody they happen to like. But no place within reach of my purse will admit Ecksteins or Blaufarbs, even as guests. The rich seem able to endure their company without defilement, but not the middle class.

The Rosenblatts have little contact with the rich; they differ in no way from the typical family at any of our moderate-priced colonies—except of course that they have more brains, and perhaps a little more money. Like the rest of us, they are solid and settled persons; their interests, social and intellectual, are our interests; their manners are our manners—or perhaps a little better; like the rest of us, they entertain a somewhat tepid respect for religion in the abstract, but seldom enter a house of worship. Yet it is enough to damn them that they are Jews. Some of our summer neighbors know the Rosenblatts in New York and keep on good terms with them—perhaps for the same reason that you would keep on good terms with your Japanese acquaintances if you lived in Manchukuo; still, they do keep on good terms with them. But once let these same people get away to the country for the summer, and they will tell you with all solemnity that the colony would be ruined if it ever began to let in Jews.

Perhaps in that "began to" lies part of the explanation, or at least of the excuse; where one Jewish family goes other Jewish families are apt to follow; as even the most Hebraeophile of Gentiles will mournfully tell you, they all have relatives. So they have, but Gentiles have relatives too, and their relatives can be extremely offensive. Also, where one Gentile family goes other Gentile families are apt to follow. You usually get into a summer colony on the recommendation of friends who have been there before, after an inspection by the proprietor or the membership committee. Friends are sometimes careless in their recommendations, and membership committees sometimes make mistakes. But when a disagreeable Gentile family gets into the colony, or Gentile neighbors make the place noisome with their intolerable relatives, people feel that this is one of the inevitable hardships of life, a cross that must be borne. Whereas a disagreeable Jewish family would evoke the comment, "Well, what can you expect of Jews?"

In the case of one settlement where we used to spend the summer, I can see some excuse for a policy of rigorous exclusion. It lies in a mountainous district which ought to be renamed the Hill Country of Judah, and the Hebrews who have chosen that part of the world for their summer resort are in the main the least pleasing specimens of their race. When you see the countryside and the market town overrun by fat women from the East Side clad in sweaters and dirty white linen shorts, the fatter the shorter, you return thankfully to the colony, a Gentile island in a Hebrew sea, and feel as if you and your neighbors were a little band of Greeks making a desperate last stand at Thermopylæ against the engulfing hordes of the Orient. Naturally enough; those Jews are not our kind of people. But they are not the Rosenblatts' kind of people either; and the Rosenblatts, by most of the tests of congeniality, are our kind. Nevertheless, the gates are barred.

Once only in its history that colony harbored a Jewish guest over the week-end. A leading resident, for some reason which I have forgotten, had to see a Jewish friend in such a hurry that he asked him out to his summer place. The visitor happened to be by far the most distinguished person who had ever visited the settlement; but his host smuggled him in as cautiously, and kept him out of sight as vigilantly, as if he had been an abolitionist of the fifties harboring a fugitive slave.

The same feeling shows itself in other places than summer colonies. Once I lived in a suburb—a typical suburb, chiefly inhabited by Aryan Protestants who were desperately clinging to the ragged edge by tooth and toenail, trying to meet the mortgage payments and keep up a front at the same time. A neighbor of mine had a bitter grievance against the real estate company, or the club committee, or somebody else in authority; and getting no satisfaction, he was driven to the awful threat, "I'll sell my house to Jews!" He could not have done it; the sort of Jews who cared to live in that suburb would not have bought his modest cottage. We had several Jewish residents, and the least opulent of them lived in a house far better than his. But to point that out to him would have been unkind, and futile. For by that time he was in a mood of homicidal and suicidal frenzy; he wanted to do the very worst thing he could think of—scuttle the ship, derail the train, blow up the powder magazine; betray the citadel, and let in the alien who would steal the palladium of Aryan exclusiveness.

II

Now any group of people may reasonably prefer to live, if they can, in the company of people of their own sort, especially when they live in the isolated intimacy of a summer colony, or even the semi-isolation and semi-intimacy of a residential suburb. To say that we want in our colony only families of the same general background as our own, families who are (or were, in the days before everybody went broke) adequately but not offensively prosperous, and sufficiently but not inconveniently intellectual—that is no more than good sense, and could give legitimate offense to nobody. But when families which meet the test in all other respects are excluded merely because they are what is called Jews, that is rather disquieting; and less disquieting to the Jew (who can always find some place to spend the summer) than to the reflective Gentile.

For what is a Jew? Wherein lies the difference that debars the Rosenblatts and their like from our summer colonies? Not in religion, surely. There may be an occasional Catholic family in these settlements, but the overwhelming majority is Protestant, in the sense that we are of Protestant background and habit of mind. But few of us go to church; and those who have any interest in organized religion give their somewhat Laodicean allegiance to Modernist Protestantism, whose differences from Reformed Judaism are infinitesimal. The religious difference would be sound reason for excluding orthodox Jews (who would not want to fellowship with us anyway), but none of the Jewish families we know is orthodox.

Nor is it a matter of race. If the evidence of history and of eye-witness observation is worth anything, the Jews are no more a race than the Germans; like every nation in modern Europe (to say nothing of America), they are a mixture of races unified by a culture in so far as they are unified at all. Even that culture is chiefly of alien and largely of Christian imposition; what people think of as traditional Jewish characteristics cannot be discerned in the Jews who appear in the first trustworthy historical passages of the Old Testament. The Jews of David's day were ignorant and bigoted farmers, exactly

like the hill-billies who made up the strength of the Ku
Klux Klan. The Phoenicians were the smart business
men of that period, and while Hiram King of Tyre com-
plained that Solomon had gypped him in a real estate
deal, that seems to have been a distinct exception. Then
and for centuries after the bulk of the Jews had the hill-
billy's distrust of the city slicker who appreciates the
amenities of life; the roars of Amos of Tekoa against
those who lie on beds of ivory, and chant to the sound
of viols, and drink wine in bowls (they used goatskin
bags, back in Tekoa) set the keynote to which rural fana-
tics have faithfully attuned their vituperations for
twenty-seven hundred years.

Judaism as we know it began with the Exile, and some
think that Hebrew business ability was learned by the
rivers of Babylon; but as late as New Testament days
the typical Palestine Jew was an ignorant and bigoted
farmer. The Jews scattered about the Roman Empire
were artisans more often than business men; the Syrian
was the shrewd trader of those times. Probably many
"Jews" of today are the descendants of converted Carthaginians, and I believe that there is a theory that Jewish
business ability dates from the annexation of that gifted
commercial race. But the most authentic Carthaginians
in the United States, the Minorcans of St Augustine,
seem to have lost those ancestral impulses; like Fafner,
they lie quiet and possess; and I do not see why traits

that died out of Christianized Carthaginians should have survived in Hebraeized Carthaginians but for Christian compulsion.

The Jews—the mixture of many races unified by the Jewish faith—became traders because medieval Christendom kept them off the land, and sharp traders because they had to be sharp to live under Christian persecution; they congregated in ghettos because Christians drove them there. If Jews are better business men than Christians, it is because the Christians compelled them to get a several hundred years' start; if they stand together, it is because the Christians taught them that in standing together lay their only tenuous hope of surviving at all.

All of this, perhaps, is irrelevant to the feeling of my summer neighbors; they are concerned with the manifestations of Jewish shrewdness and solidarity, not with its origins. The point is that these manifestations have all but disappeared from the Jews we know. Jews are still apt to stand together under persecution, mild and severe; you cannot easily eradicate the habit of fifteen centuries. But with the ghetto a dimming memory, with Jewish orthodoxy (in this country, at least) fading as fast as Christian orthodoxy, the only unifying influences are tradition and culture. And they are far weaker than the average Gentile may think.

In New York City there are two million Jews who may in moments of excitement think of themselves as all

Jews together; but only in moments of excitement. In between times, the Spanish-Portuguese Jews who came (mostly from Holland) in the seventeenth century snoot the German and Alsatian Jews who came in the early nineteenth century; and they both snoot the Russian Jews who came in the later nineteenth century; and they all get together to snoot the Levantine Jews who arrived in the early years of the twentieth century—these last being, ironically enough, the distant cousins of the Spanish-Portuguese Jews of the top layer. It merely happened that one lot went east and the other north when Torquemada drove them out of Spain; but talk to a member of the Congregation Shearith Israel about his Levantine brethren down on Rivington Street, and you are likely to get as frigid a look as if you talked to an Irish Catholic about his brethren the Polish Catholics— or to a French Catholic of the old stock about his brethren the Irish Catholics.

There is of course an immense cultural difference between the typical member of the Congregation Shearith Israel and the typical Levantine Jew of Rivington Street (though one of the most useful citizens I ever knew was a Levantine Jew from Rivington Street). What made that difference? They are both Jews, and Jews of the same tribe; they have enjoyed without interruption the same Jewish culture. The difference is that for four hundred years they were exposed to different Gentile cultures; in the one case the culture of Holland and America, in the other the culture of the decadent Turkish Empire.

Now the culture that is molding all middle-class Manhattan today is the local culture of an island metropolis, little understood and still less liked by the hinterland. Where a man came from, and which of the countless races represented in New York supplied his ancestry, is a matter of less importance to most of us than our common interests and our common habits of mind. This is true of almost all New Yorkers of Protestant background, of almost all Jews who have escaped from the ghetto tradition; of most of the Catholics who do not carry their Catholicism to the point of making a religion of it. The dominant influences that shape the Rosenblatts are the same that shape the Smiths and the O'Gradys; and it seems irrational that a summer colony which admits the Smiths and the O'Gradys should keep the Rosenblatts out.

And, finally, my summer neighbors cannot be accused of anti-Semitism in the ordinary sense of that word; they are as indignant as anybody at the behavior of the Hitlerites; they abhor the idea of persecution of Jews, of discrimination against Jews in business, professions, public life. But they will not have Jewish neighbors, even if the Jews are in all perceptible respects like themselves.

The one imperceptible but decisive difference is that Jews are Jews, whatever that means, and we are Aryan Protestants, even though our Aryanism is theoretical and our Protestantism vestigial. Ask any of us, and we would admit that Aryan Protestants are the salt of the earth; though we should not say so without being asked. That would be vulgar boasting; also we feel that the fact is self-evident. So Irish Catholics feel in their bones the superiority of Irish Catholics, Russian Jews of Russian Jews, Turkish Moslems of Turkish Moslems. It is a healthy way to feel—so long as you are really convinced of your superiority and do not try to prove it by the offensive arrogance which is the symptom of the inferiority complex.

As arrogance goes, the exclusion of Jews, agreeable as well as disagreeable, from summer colonies is a not very offensive variety; but I am afraid it is an unmistakable symptom none the less.

III

Being an Aryan Protestant, I am as firmly convinced of the high merit of Aryan Protestants as anybody; indeed rather more confident of the merit of Aryanism than are the Nazis. I am so sure of it that I feel no need to prove it by breaking the windows of Jewish stores, or to insist that I must not be exposed to the competition of

Jews in my profession. And the reasons, aside from in-herited prejudice? Well, the virtue of the Aryan (granted that he is only an ideal abstraction) is that he looks the universe in the eye and tries to do some-thing about it, instead of bending submissively before the inevitable. And the virtue of the Protestant (how-ever individual Protestants or Protestant churches may have sinned against the Holy Ghost) is insistence on the right to think things out for himself, and acceptance of personal responsibility for the consequences.

The Catholic, the orthodox Jewish, the Moslem way of life, each has its special virtues, and no doubt the human race needs them all; but we should not be even as human as we are, we should not have much hope of ever getting anywhere in the future, without the contri-butions of Aryan Protestantism to world culture. That is why I hate Adolf Hitler and his followers as no Jew can ever hate them; they have made Aryan virtues ridic-ulous.

The Germans profess to be the most Aryan of Aryans. "Nordic blood represents that Mystery which has re-placed and vanquished the ancient sacrifice," says a gentleman now high in the German government, named (somewhat surprisingly) Rosenberg. But since there are Gentile Cohans and Leavys in Ireland, there may well be Aryan Rosenbergs in Germany. You would suppose that sixty-odd million Aryans endowed with this in-

vincible holiness would not need to be afraid of six
hundred thousand Jews, but they are. When, before
the Nazis had captured the government, their strong-
arm men swept down the Kurfürstendamm in Berlin
one Passover, beating up all Jews or suspected Jews,
you would expect that each of these Aryan heroes, strong
in his self-conscious superiority, would attack twenty
Semites. Not so; twenty Aryans ganged on a single Jew.

Mr Edgar Ansel Mowrer, from whose *Germany Puts
the Clock Back* I draw these edifying instances, observes
that Jews have been living in Germany—and the most
civilized parts of Germany at that—certainly since the
Dark Ages and probably since Roman days; by history,
habit, and cultural environment they are more "German"
than most of the Junkers east of the Elbe who consider
themselves super-Germans. But this does not matter to
the Aryans, who fall back on the unverifiable criterion of
race, and prove their manly strength by beating the
enemy into submission—a carefully selected enemy
whom they outnumber a hundred to one. This is the
inferiority complex at its very worst.

But of course the Jews are a dangerous lot, a race of
diabolical cleverness—if you believe the Germans. Well,
if the average Jew is more clever and more intellectual
than the average Christian, the Christians have only
themselves to blame; they compelled the Jews to earn
their living by their brains through several centuries in

which Christians made their living by wielding (according to their respective social stations) the sword or the hoe. But it seems that the Jews have an even worse vice. They are eternal aliens, unassimilable—the tapeworm in the organism, as the well-remembered Count Reventlow delicately puts it. Their racial-religious culture has such vitality that no surrounding culture can dissolve or even dilute it.

If this is so, the Jews do not know it and never have known it. All Jewish history, down to the triumph of Christianity, resounds with complaints that Jews would not be Jews if they had a chance to be anything else. King Solomon married some goy wives, and immediately began to be what would nowadays be called an assimilationist. So did King Ahab, a hundred and fifty years later. Those were early and simple days; but presently the prophets developed the concept of a peculiar and chosen people, the favorite of the one God of all the earth. It followed that this people's culture, rooted in true religion, was superior to all other cultures; and it was a source of bitter annoyance to the prophets that Jews exposed to any other culture usually wanted to try it.

Even after the Exile and the Return had confirmed the Chosen Remnant in its conviction that it was the salt of the earth, Jewish boys took to marrying goy girls from Ashdod, Ammon, Moab; and Jewish culture was apparently as much imperiled by these Gentile influences as

German culture is alleged to be imperiled by Jewish influences. The pious Nehemiah had to use Nazi methods to get his people back on the right track. "I contended with them, and cursed them, and smote certain of them, and plucked off their hair. And one of the sons of Joiada, the son of Eliashib the high priest, was son-in-law to Sanballat the Horonite; therefore I chased him from me. Remember them, O my God, because they have defiled the priesthood. Remember me, O my God, for good."

But the tendency seemed ineradicable. Jewish culture had managed to escape engulfment in Phoenician culture, Babylonian culture, Philistine culture; but it pretty nearly succumbed to Greek culture. A high priest of the Seleucid period "built a place of exercise, and brought the chief young men under his subjection, and made them wear a hat. Now such was the height of Greek fashions that the priests had no courage to serve any more at the altar; but despising the temple, and neglecting the sacrifices, hastened to be partakers of the unlawful allowance in the place of exercise, after the game of discus called them forth." What is the self-conscious superiority of God's chosen people, compared to the Gentile joys of throwing the discus and wearing a hat? Luckily there was raised up Judas Maccabaeus, the Hitler of his day, who rallied the hill-billies and saved the old-time religion.

It is one of the great achievements of Christianity that it managed to stamp out this inclination of the Jews not to be Jews if they could help it. For more than a thousand years before the Christians got control of the secular arm assimilation had repeatedly menaced the very existence of Judaism; but when Jews had no choice but to remain Jews or turn Christian they preferred to go on being Jews, even at the risk of expropriation, torture, and the stake. For fifteen hundred years they remained steadfast in their allegiance to their own culture; but when Christianity began to weaken, the old assimilationist tendencies revived. Many Jews even turned Christian when they were no longer in danger of being burned alive for not turning Christian. They were still God's chosen people, the salt of the earth; but when at last they could exercise freedom of choice without sacrificing their self-respect, many of them chose to discard their unique privileges and do what was being done by the best people around them. And this is what German philosophers call "the eternal Jew."

IV

If Jews no longer turn Christian, it is because the best people are no longer as a rule conspicuous for Christian devotion; but assimilation to a rationalist or indifferent Gentile culture is going on as fast as in the days just before Judas Maccabaeus. New York has hundreds of thousands of Jews who are still living in ghetto conditions and are not yet rid of the ghetto psychology; but it also has thousands of Jewish families who are virtually indistinguishable from their Gentile neighbors. In the arts, and the businesses ancillary to the arts, the assimilation is already practically complete.

This, in a city so largely Jewish, is a two-way assimilation; it means the evolution of a local culture containing elements of both Jewish and Gentile origin. To me, an Aryan Protestant, that seems a gratifying development; the people who froth at the mouth about it are not, as a rule, the self-conscious Gentiles, but the self-conscious Jews, the spiritual descendants of Nehemiah. Much has been written about the Jewish inferiority complex, but its social manifestations are merely the sort of thing you will always see when a lately submerged social class is winning its way to wealth and power. The really serious and sickening displays of the Jewish inferiority complex are offered by people of a much higher order. The fanatical Jewish super-patriot who goes around with a chip on his shoulder, insisting not only that Jews are superior to Gentiles but that Gentiles must acknowledge that superiority, who sets people down as anti-Semitic merely because they do not like him personally—where is the difference between him and the Nazi? It is greatly to the credit of the mass of intelligent Jews that they have perceived, sooner than the mass of intelligent people of other tribes, that no culture has a monopoly of merit; and that to claim a monopoly for your own is only to make yourself ridiculous.

It is an abrupt descent, perhaps, from the megalo-maniac enthusiasms and noble rages of the German Nazis and their Jewish similars to the somewhat pallid preferences and antipathies of my summer neighbors. The difference in degree is enormous, because my neigh-bors are more kindly than Hitler or Nehemiah—and also, I fear, more ineffectual; but it is only a difference in degree, not in kind. Its implications are most unflatter-ing to Aryan Protestants and its practical consequences are most unfortunate for society.

For the natural reaction of a Jew who has practically stopped being a Jew, who feels no difference between himself and his Protestant neighbors, and then discovers that those neighbors are still conscious of an ineffaceable difference—his natural reaction is to go back to being a Jew, and a rather fanatical Jew at that. Many Jews, to their great credit, resist this impulse and wait for the slow attrition of time to bring the Protestants to their senses; but others decide that if the surrounding and pre-dominantly Gentile culture in which they feel them-selves merging spews them forth, if they are compelled to flock with people of their discarded ancestral faith rather than with people of their own kind, they had

better make a virtue of necessity and argue that Jews
are the only people fit to flock with, that any Jew is *ipso*
facto superior to any Gentile. The argument is quite
as rational as that any Gentile is *ipso facto* superior to
any Jew; but few modernized Jews would ever make it
if they were not driven to it.

This middle-class Protestant exclusiveness is hamper-
ing and delaying—though I do not believe it can permanently prevent—an assimilation which is important
for the well being of American society, and vitally important for the well being of the metropolitan society
of New York. But quite as unfortunate is the light it
throws on the mentality of Aryan Protestants. If we were
so sure of our superiority should we be afraid to expose
it to comparison? The rich and great, in the main, have
more self-assurance. Those of them who compose the
residue of what used to be called Society may often prefer
not to fellowship with Hebrews; but those whose riches
and greatness depend on what they have done themselves, not what their ancestors did, are more likely to
impose no criterion but personal congeniality.

But my friends and summer neighbors are not the rich
and great. They are good people—kindly, pleasant, useful; but it would be rather hard for them to claim any
special superiority on visible and tangible evidence. If
they must be superior, as apparently they must, they
can be so only through setting up by implication—of

course they would never put it so crudely—the doctrine that middle-class Aryan Protestants are automatically gentlefolk, and Jews of the same class are not. The definition of a gentleman is a debatable matter, which need not be gone into here; it need only be said that I know of no definition which would include all my Gentile friends and exclude all my Jewish friends unless you set up this unarguable delimitation by creed and race.

I think better of Aryan Protestantism than that; we have our peculiar virtues and we need not be afraid of comparisons. But the Protestant habit of mind has one disastrous weakness, as evident in ex-Protestant rationalists as in those who still keep the faith—the tendency to quarrel most bitterly with those who are most like us but not quite like us, instead of sinking our trivial differences and standing together against those who are not like us at all. (The early Church had the same failing, before Catholic doctrine was defined and solidified by the great Councils.) Middle-class reformed Jews or ex-Jews are almost exactly like us; if we really believe that we are the salt of the earth we ought to welcome them, assimilate them, instead of drawing a line on scientifically untenable grounds and driving them back into fellowship with people who are not like us in the least.

But the Aryan Protestant is afraid—secretly, often unconsciously, afraid; afraid that his race and his faith are dying out. Bewildered and alarmed, he can think of no defensive measure but to keep to himself as far as possible, preserve himself from the contaminating presence of more devout and more prolific breeds. I believe his fears are exaggerated; evidence on birth rates seems to show that fecundity decreases, whether automatically or by voluntary action, as any class improves its economic status—and this despite the thunders of a religion which on this one point still has some aid from the secular arm. Also, the Protestant middle-class would have more children if it were part of a sanely organized society which guaranteed some security for people who were willing to work; and I am optimist enough to believe, even in such times as these, that there is a chance that our children may live in that sort of society.

As for the fading of our faith, Modernist Protestantism and Reformed Judaism are both half-way houses—wayside tourist camps for those who are on the way out from orthodoxy to complete freedom of thought, but do not feel strong enough to make the whole trip all at once. It would seem not only more intelligent but more fraternal, even more Christian, to make friends with our fellow-travelers; they may have come from a different starting point but their destination is the same as our own. The Modernist clergy do this, of course, but few of their parishioners seem willing to follow them. Yet Jewish orthodoxy is disappearing more rapidly than Christian orthodoxy; and the Jews we meet in the half-way house may some day be useful and needed allies, if the present tribulation continues and begins to drive the weaker brethren back to the Everlasting Arms.

I do not suppose my summer neighbors perceive all these far-reaching implications of their insistence that the Rosenblatts must not be asked down for the week-end; but the implications are inescapable once you set any criterion but that of personal congeniality. When you do that you say that we are the people, the salt of the earth, not by reason of our achievements, our tastes, our reactions, but simply in virtue of an ancestral creed that most of us have discarded, and a racial inheritance that is largely mythical. Against the exclusion, from colonies that ought to be like-minded and harmonious, of offensive Jews (or offensive Gentiles) I have no objection. But when you say that people who are like us in tastes, ideas, and manners must not be allowed to pollute the holy place even for a week-end, then you are descending to the ghetto psychology without the ghetto's excuse.

But I am afraid this reasoning will have no effect on my Aryan friends. In the cities where they live in the winter they are not perceptibly superior persons; they live where they can and as they can, and they are likely to be outshone by their Jewish neighbors. (Unintentionally outshone, quite often; but that makes it all the worse.) But they must demonstrate their superiority in some way, and summer gives them their chance. They flock by themselves in aboriginal reservations, Aryan ghettos, to which any decently presentable Gentile who looks as if he could pay his rent can gain admission—provided he understands that he may have no Jewish guests.

Some of my Jewish friends are rather hurt by all this; which, after all, is more flattering than if they merely laughed.

On Being Kept by a Cat

ON BEING KEPT BY A CAT

THE lamented Freddie Mortimer of the New York *Times* was once moved to scorn by an item among the Lost and Found notices—an advertisement for a lost cat whose collar bore the inscription, "This is So-and-so's cat." Nothing, Mortimer contended, could be less accurate; the only identification that could truthfully be inscribed on any cat's collar would be, "This is this cat's cat."

For the gentleman who thought he owned the cat, not quite so much could be said. Madame Michelet (quoted by the learned Van Vechten, whose *The Tiger in the House* is practically the *Golden Bough* of cat lore) once computed that she had owned a hundred cats. "Say rather," her husband corrected, "that a hundred cats have owned you." Possibly he was jealous of the creatures who had usurped his rightful place as the domestic pet, but anybody with much feline experience knows he was right—especially people who do not keep servants, and must refuse invitations for week-ends because somebody has to stay at home to take care of the member of the family who cannot open ice-box doors. To the question often asked by the inexpert, "Do you keep a cat?" the proper answer is "No, a cat keeps me."

It is true that the courts have held that a cat is property, an opinion not concurred in by certain resort hotels which will take a cat for a dollar a day European plan; they make no such charge for your trunk. This seems to be one of the many instances in which business is more realistic than the law; the theory that a cat is property must be set down as one of those splendid flights of wishful thinking in which judges occasionally indulge. It would be pleasant to believe that somebody who is broke and looking for a job has equal power in contracting for wages with a prospective employer, so the courts have often held that this is so; it would be agreeable to a judge who is not used to having his injunctions disregarded to believe that the most independent of all creatures is subject to human control. But the doctrine breaks down under analysis.

Scholarly and subtle men have written much of late about the distinctions between various kinds of property. There are consumption goods—clothes, for instance—which we all possess; and there the means of production which are owned by capitalists, but owned in different ways. I am, in economic terminology, a handicraft artisan owning my own means of production—a typewriter, with which I earn my living; I am also on an infinitesimal scale a capitalist. But my "ownership" of, say 1/435,000th part of the General Motors Corporation does not enable me to do anything with that tiny fraction of a great institution except to sell it if I choose. Henry Ford owns and uses the Ford Motor Company as I own and use my typewriter; but all I "own" in General Motors is a claim on a little of its profit, if men over whose actions I have no control manage it well enough to make a profit.

Obviously, the cat who for some years has made his home with my family falls into none of what I must apologize for calling these categories of property. He is not consumption goods but a consumer, and a fairly heavy consumer at that; nor does he produce anything except an intense satisfaction in those who associate with him. Nothing else of utility to human beings, at least; he makes what a cat doubtless regards as profits, and seems to think I have a claim on a share of them. Whenever he kills a mouse in the apartment, or a snake at his summer home in the country, he proudly brings it back to the family, perhaps supposing that we might like to eat some of it. But even then I stand in much the same economic relation to him as to Mr Alfred P. Sloan.

Reverse the situation, and the true property relation becomes apparent. I am to the cat what my typewriter is to me, or the Ford Motor Company to Henry Ford—his means of production; in the course of time he will eat up all the money I get for these observations.* If he is not my sole proprietor, at least he owns enough stock in me to make his wishes influential; and as for the members of the family who do most of the work of caring for him, he seems to regard them as his employees. If they do not work for him as and when he wants them to work he expresses his opinion—though more politely than Mr Tom Girdler expresses his opinion in a similar situation.

This economic analysis of course does not apply to the alley cat, the free-lance cat who earns his living by his own exertions without exploiting the labor of others. But the house cat, the pet cat, so far from being property, is a capitalist, a member of the owner class, even if he catches a mouse now and then for sport. His mousing is comparable to the farming practiced by retired gentlemen of wealth, who do for amusement what their ancestors did because they had to. And when so many people are asking what the capitalist gives in return for what he gets, the cat too must stand examination.

———

* So he will—but not that particular money, only its equivalent. As it turned out the entire family ate for a couple of months on the proceeds of this commentary, at a time when no other income was coming in. That summer, we undeniably were kept by a cat. Thus proving, as will be set forth later, that any cat can be a producer when the situation requires.

II

"Probably the least useful of domestic animals," was the verdict of C. E. Browne and the late G. Stanley Hall, writing in the *Pedagogical Seminary;* which implies a very narrow concept of utility. The cat does not produce material wealth, nor acquire it unless he has to; and even then no more than he needs. But was Rembrandt the least useful of Dutchmen, or Bach of Germans? What Bach and Rembrandt produced (from the point of view of the sociologist, if not of the economist) was pleasure in others, and pleasure of a high order. That is what the cat produces too—the pleasure that comes from observing in many cats an astonishing beauty, and in practically all cats the perfection of grace; the still higher pleasure derived from contemplation of the most dignified and independent of living creatures. Tiberius Gracchus so admired the cat's independence that he put an image of a cat in the Temple of Liberty at Rome, as freedom's best symbol; at least so say Hall and Browne—Plutarch does not mention it. I do not know the explanation of Lenin's well-known fondness for cats; but perhaps he got an ironic satisfaction from the companionship of the only beings in Russia whom he could not boss.

The independence of course is far more conspicuous

in alley cats, the most vigorous of all practitioners, in a civilized environment, of private initiative and rugged individualism. This ought to make the alley cat the favorite animal of the conservative rich; yet I suspect that if you took a census of these gentry you would find that most of them prefer the docile dog; their definition of individualism is usually "individualism for me." The cat, on the other hand, seems to be widely preferred by artists and writers—a tribe which with rare exceptions is almost fanatically individualistic, and values individualism and independence in its friends, human or animal.

But any cat is a potential alley cat; the most pampered of domestic pets could get along on his own if he had to. My cat (the possessive is used, here and hereinafter, purely for identification) is a silver Persian, who in his urban apartment leads a placid and sedentary life for nine months of the year. But when he goes to the country in June he is perfectly at home in woods and fields, and fights everything in sight. The cat's high sense of enlightened self-interest leads him to live on his income if he can—but because it is pleasanter, not because he must. The tendency is not unknown among human beings.

Besides the free-lance alley cat and the capitalistic house cat there is a third economic group—the salaried cats, in public or private employ. Mostly they are maintained to keep down rats and mice, though in wartime many served in the trenches or in submarines, to give gas alarms. In this class there are economic gradations, just as among human salaried employees; I suppose that from the feline point of view cats employed in meat markets rank highest—the movie stars or corporation presidents of the cat world. They experience all the vicissitudes of salaried employees too; lately the Mayor of Boston, in a drive for economy, slashed the salaries of the cats employed in the Public Library from $10 a year apiece to $9.85, for which relief Boston taxpayers were presumably grateful.

The cat makes the best of any situation in which he finds himself, but he is shrewd enough as a rule to prefer the pleasanter modes of life; I have known alley cats so jealous of their independence that they refused employment in groceries, but such resolution is rare. An illustration is the history of my friend Amos, a big brindle tom who used to live with an elderly couple in New York. The husband died, the wife decided to give up housekeeping and go live with her children, who for some reason had no room for Amos; so she put him in the Bide-a-Wee Home pending adoption. It happened that about that time a certain club discovered to its horror that there were rats in the basement, and the Board of Governors empowered the manager to add a cat to the payroll. He went to the Bide-a-Wee Home, saw Amos and admired him (as who would not?) and employed him—after an exchange of references; for the lady who had been associated with Amos wanted to be sure that he joined the right club. Amos came, looked around, and evidently decided that this was not the club for him. The next day he vanished; but six weeks later he reappeared, looking somewhat bedraggled, and has been there ever since.

So far as the history of that interlude can be reconstructed, Amos went back home and discovered that home was not there any more; whereupon he decided to become an alley cat. He evidently succeeded in supporting himself by free-lancing; but like many a human being in the same situation, he finally concluded that it was too much of a strain and he had better go back to a salaried job; the job at the club might not be just what he wanted, but if it was the best proposition in sight he might as well take it. By now Amos enjoys club life; he knows the most comfortable chairs, and any of his fellow-members who dared to turn him out of his seat would hear from the House Committee. And he certainly earns his salary. Soon he had killed the last rat in the basement; then he began visiting the club across the street and killing their rats, proudly bringing them back to his own club to show that he was on the job. And now that both clubs are thoroughly deratted he has added the bank round the corner to his territory—appearing every morning as soon as it opens, with a face that asks the clearly legible question, "Any rats today? Anything a cat can do around here?"

Amos, it is obvious, has the instinct of workmanship, the delight in doing a job for its own sake; but he preferred the ease of the old home so long as he could get it. The American dream of the workman turning capitalist, and living in comfort without working any more, was familiar to every cat before America was ever heard of.

III

For the house cat has known better days, which may still linger in his racial memory; in Egypt he was once a god. Not that by any means all domestic cats of today are of Egyptian ancestry, any more than all Southerners are descended from the great ante-bellum plantation owners. But every Southerner literate enough to know the tradition cherishes the memory of the old white-pillared mansion that was burned by Sherman's army; and so it may be that every cat, even if all his ancestors came from Central Europe, likes to think that once his people were gods in Egypt.

The cat race, with its Manx and Siamese and Persian and all the other varieties, plainly has as many different kinds of ancestors as the German "race." The long-haired cats, the experts are inclined to think, are de-

scended from the manul of Central Asia. I know this
creature only from photographs, but he seems to have a
formidable, even menacing dignity that would have
made him a good playmate for Genghis Khan. As for
short-haired cats, they come down from various wild
species, European, Asiatic, African, and even American;
there were domesticated cats in Mexico and Central
America before the first Europeans came.

But the cat as a domestic institution of Western Culture first arose in Egypt, where there was a temple to
the cat-goddess at Bubastis as early as 1500 B. C. Long
before that Egyptian mythology told of the Great Cat,
the celestial cat who kills the snake that sometimes tries
to swallow the sun. (Those who remember one of the
late Bert Williams's most famous stories will suspect
that his name was Martin.) It is fairly certain that the
first house cats in Europe were imported from Egypt—
probably smuggled out, since the Egyptians did not like
to let the sacred animals go. (Diodorus reports that in
the days of Egyptian imperialism, armies campaigning
abroad used to gather up all the cats they met and send
them back to Egypt, where they would be treated with
the proper respect.) It was in Egypt that the Greeks
first encountered the cat—the *ailouros* they called him,
the tail waver; and it is as an Egyptian animal, though
apparently not unknown to Greek readers, that he is
first mentioned in European literature, by Herodotus.

Soon after Herodotus's day cats appeared in both Greece and Italy. Richard Engelmann, in the annual of the Imperial German Archaeological Institute, mentions an Athenian vase of the classic period with a picture of a boy going to school, and his pedagogue (the accompanying slave) holding a cat on a leash. Italian vases of a not much later date show women playing with cats who look just like the cats of today. But apparently, says Engelmann, the exportation from Egypt was difficult and dangerous; cats in Europe were rare till the Christian era—and not long after that they ceased to be gods in Egypt.

When they fell they fell a long way—as far as Lucifer. In Christian Europe cats, particularly black cats, had the misfortune to be regarded as incarnations of the devil; and some people cannot get rid of that superstition to this day, though no doubt they would furiously deny that their dislike of cats is a hangover from witch-fearing ancestors. "Probably no other domestic animal," wrote Hall and Browne, "has been so loved and hated, so petted and persecuted." Even now, few people are neutral about cats; and a good deal of exaggeration can be found in arguments both for them and against them. There are people who have an instinctive horror of all cats—probably an atavistic memory of the great cats of the primal jungle, comparable to the much more common horror of snakes; there are those who cannot forget their demonology; and there are those who say they hate cats because they love dogs. You may like both of course; but people who crave the dog's uncritical devotion and are afraid to meet the coolly detached judgment of the cat, who does not like you unless he finds you worthy of liking, are making a damning admission. Leaving aside all these pathological types, people who say they dislike all cats have simply happened to know the wrong cats.

Not all cats are admirable any more than they are all detestable. "Each individual cat," says Van Vechten, "differs in as many ways as possible from each other individual cat." This may be too sweeping, but generalizations about all cats are as rash as generalizations about all human beings. All cats have tails? Not the Manx cats. All cats have fur? There were hairless cats in Aztec Mexico. Still less can you generalize about the character of "the cat." I have been well acquainted with some fifteen or twenty tail wavers; the majority were admirable—for character or intelligence or both; but several of them were disagreeable or even stupid. My present feline associate, General Gray (known to his intimates by a variety of other names as well), was given to the family (by the wife of a biped General Gray) as replacement for a cat who had been killed. He is one of the best I have ever known, but so was his predecessor; and a cat replaces another cat only to the extent that a wife replaces another wife. She may fill the same place in the household, but you have to get used to an utterly different personality. And those who know cats tend to judge them by the same criteria as human friends. I am ashamed to admit that probably the most intelligent cat I ever knew elicited my respect but not my affection. She was industrious, clever, virtuous; but she lacked charm.

Hall and Browne analyzed the results of a questionnaire in which eight hundred school children told why they liked cats; reasoning that as children anthropomorphize cats and so did primitive men, they might get some light on the early relations of the two species. (As a matter of fact only very young children, or those who do not know cats well, anthropomorphize them.) Most of the children were sure the cat loved them, not just his home, and they were probably right; to anyone who knows cats, the dogma of cat haters that the cat is attached only to places, not to persons, is a malignant myth. He likes places but he can feel great affection for persons too—affection as disinterested as human affections are likely to be. (This is true of most cats anyway; nothing is true of all cats.) *

---

* The infinite variety of feline behavior is even better known to me than when this was written; for magazine publication of this monograph, in *Harper's* and the *Reader's Digest,* brought me three or four times as much fan mail as anything else I ever wrote—even in those magazines, which seem to be a combina-

Van Vechten truly observes that "walking is distasteful to the cat unless he has a purpose in view"; but all one summer General Gray accompanied my then small daughter on her evening walks—long walks, some of them—with no purpose in view but the enjoyment of her company. Once in a while when I am working he comes in and rolls for me—not because he wants anything, but because he feels that high contentment which a cat can express only by rolling. He could roll wherever he happened to be; I can think of no reason for his coming from another room to roll in my office, except that he feels so happy that he wants to share his happiness with me.

Most of the eight hundred children said they liked cats because they were nice to play with, only a few because they were intelligent; children are apt to value their human elders by the same standard. As for the intellectuals who admire cats for their intelligence, their philosophic disposition, cat haters would say that this is precisely the same as the children's reaction. Each group reads into the cat the qualities it most appreciates, whether he really has them or not. In some cases this is

tion peculiarly adapted to evoking comment from readers. If I had collated all the information offered by my correspondents I could easily have written a book on cats; but none of the evidence necessitated any change in the general conclusions here set down.

true. People who are devoted to any pet incline to exaggerate its cleverness; less of that nonsense has been talked about cats than about babies. But many cat stories that seem absurd to ailourophobes are plausible enough to anybody who knows cats, as those who hate them do not. The Associated Press lately seemed to find an element of romance in the story of a cat in Maine which had lost a leg in a trap. His human associate fitted him with a wooden peg—and must have fitted him well, for any cat would spend hours trying to get that sort of contraption off before he ventured to walk on it; and when the cat caught a rat he held it down with his other forepaw and beat it to death with his wooden leg. Fiction? Not wholly. He may have killed the rat, eventually, with his teeth; but any cat who caught a rat would slap it round a bit, and it would be a natural muscular reflex to swing on it with the arm that happened to have a wooden peg attached.

Stories of cats' manipulative skill about the house may also be exaggerated, but there is more in them than those ignorant of the species may realize. E. L. Thorndike, the psychologist, has been scornful of this type of cat story. Thousands of cats, he says, have gone to the door, found it shut, and turned away frustrated, without getting any publicity; but let one single cat reach up and paw the door knob, and immediately he figures in all the books on animal intelligence. Maybe so; but most cats understand how a door is opened even if they cannot do it themselves. A good many cats are either naturally imitative, or else clever enough to try what they have seen human beings attempt with success. I know a cat who dials the telephone, but that is probably mere imitation; her family does not pretend that she has ever lifted the receiver off the hook or actually succeeded in getting a number.

But sometimes it looks like imitation in the hope of success. My cat has never tried to turn a door knob; he can pull a screen door open from outside, with his claws, but when he comes to a wooden door that is closed he simply sits down and scratches at the crack. (He never scratches at the wrong crack, the one where the hinges are.) Experience has taught him that sometimes the door is off the latch, in which case he can pull it open—and also that if he says he wants to get out, and any of the human members of the family are present, the door is likely to be opened for him. He likes to drink water out of the bathtub; if somebody runs a little for him he drinks as much as he wants and then pulls out the plug. That may be the accidental result of a mere impulse to play with a shiny chain; but it seems plausible that he has seen other people pull the plug when they are through with the water in the bathtub, and knows what will happen if he pulls it.

This is no proof of any great mechanical skill in even

this one particular cat, to say nothing of the entire species; it is merely observed evidence of more general intelligence than enemies of the cats are willing to admit. Some of them indeed admit almost nothing—not even those reflective qualities for which the cat is most esteemed by connoisseurs.

IV

The most vigorous attempt to debunk the cat which has come to my attention—its unfavorable conclusions all buttressed by laboratory experiment—is a book published in 1928 by Georgina Gates, then assistant professor at Barnard College, entitled *The Modern Cat: a Study in Comparative Psychology.* Perhaps none of the science of that romantic year need be taken too seriously; much of the physics of 1928 seems to be only antique heresy now, while as for the economics of 1928—! However, let the cat answer the indictment, which is comprehensive enough. The cat has few ideas; she "sees no colors, distinguishes no pitches"; objects are ill defined to her, she "lives in a blur," with no memories and no anticipations. "She is no philosopher," says Dr Gates, "no mechanician, no student or critic of human affairs; merely a distant relative, poverty-stricken with respect to the most valuable of all possessions, but cherished for her air of aloofness and that aura of mystery which surrounds her." In short, a poor relation of our noble species.

Now with all respect to the scientific approach, this seems to me to betray very little knowledge of cats outside the laboratory; and it anthropomorphizes the cat more thoroughly than do even the youngest children. It implies that what is useful or pleasant to us must be useful or pleasant to cats too, and that they are deficient in so far as they lack it. The cat is condemned for not being a successful human being. How many human beings could be successful cats?

Certain experiments are cited as proof that the cat is tone-deaf and color-blind. Color blindness is a considerable misfortune to men and women but much less serious for the cat, who does not have to watch traffic lights; who has other senses to help him distinguish objects and other pleasures to replace those which color gives us. The charge of tone-deafness rests on the researches of an earnest investigator who found that cats could not distinguish (or at least did not find it worth while to show that they distinguished) between different notes on the piano. So what? Why should a cat be interested in the notes of the piano? When he wants music he makes his own.

Anybody who knows cats outside the laboratory knows that their hearing is far superior to ours. Even if they cannot distinguish between the notes of the piano (I remain unconvinced of that), they can detect and identify countless sounds too faint for the human ear, or too obscure for the human understanding. The widespread belief that cats are "psychic" is partly a residue of old superstition, but partly it rests on the observed fact that cats are sensitive to certain impressions which human senses miss. Probably their better hearing is responsible for most of this, their sensitiveness to electricity for the rest of it—a sense which most human beings wholly lack. In the sense of smell the cat's superiority is still greater. It tells him much that we learn by sight, much that we get by conversation or reading, and probably some things we never get at all. Those who despise the cat for his alleged insensitiveness to notes of the piano might ask themselves what he would say of a species so dull, so crude, so poverty-stricken that its language actually has no word for the nasal equivalent of color-blindness;* which is as insensitive to the innumerable delicate distinctions of scent that the cat perceives as he may (or may not) be to the different tones of musical instruments.

"The cat lives in a blur," does he? Well, he does not act in a blur; when he has something to do, somewhere to go, he goes and does it with speed and precision. At

---

* Rodman Gilder suggests that this blank in our vocabulary be filled by the euphonious monosyllable "snoof."

a distance, in broad daylight, his vision is probably less precise than ours; but he identifies such objects, and at such distances, as his needs require, by the coordination of other senses. And at night—! Stumble over a cat in the dark and he will be surprised, though unless you step on a foot or a tail he will be too courteous to express indignation. Turn on the light, and you can read in his eyes as much pity and disdain for a poor creature who cannot see in the dark as scientists feel for a poor creature who does not know (or care about) the difference between G sharp and B flat. Dr Gates remarks that if you put a cat in front of a mirror he will not recognize his own reflection, probably will not realize that this is the image of a cat. Which is true. But if there is another cat, a strange cat, near by the chances are that he will know it before you do; certainly he will if the other cat is around a corner, or if it is dark.

Most of this depreciation of the cat is sheer anthropomorphizing. We have enormously developed one sense at the expense of all the rest; by far the greater part of the material used by the human mind is collected, in one way or another, by the eye. Unfavorable judgments on the cat's perceptive powers by members of a species whose other senses are far weaker (in the case of smell, almost atrophied) are as uninformed, as uncomprehending, in short as worthless, as the ideas of a celibate on matrimony.

Nobody who knows cats believes that they have no memories or anticipations; they remember and anticipate much that we do not care about and are indifferent to much that interests us; but why not? It is their business to be cats, ours to be human. But what about the most valuable of all possessions, in which the cat is said to be so poverty-stricken? This is reasoning power; the cat's deficiency in which is proved, to Dr Gates's satisfaction, by one of Thorndike's experiments. He took twelve alley cats, put them before a complicated set of boxes to find a devious way to food, and timed them. Only one found the way easily; as a group they were faster than raccoons, but slower than monkeys or Columbia students.

One must respect the findings of a properly conducted experiment, but need not accept all the conclusions drawn from it. Any educated alley cat (and those who learn slowly die young) knows that food comes in garbage cans, not in trick boxes. Confronted with a novel situation, food in an unfamiliar container, the cats were slow to adapt themselves to their environment. But it does not appear that Thorndike was so inhumane as to push them to the verge of starvation; if he had, probably every one of those cats would have got the food before it starved, which after all is the passing grade for an alley cat. Finding one's way out of mechanical complications is, it must be remembered, more of a human than a feline necessity; and more of a human (or, as the experiment suggests, a simian) aptitude.

But the unfavorable conclusions were based chiefly on the way the cats went at it; they pawed round apparently at random, sometimes trying the wrong way over and over. "Man learns, the cat scrambles," Dr Gates concludes; but she admits that a Columbia professor who did not know how to swim, if he fell into so unfamiliar an environment as deep water, would flounder as awkwardly as Thorndike's cats. "The cat uses man's second-best procedure, hit-or-miss struggling," instead of coolly, patiently reasoning his way out. How many men do any better? Pick up the first twelve human beings you meet, put them into a human situation of equivalent novelty and complexity, and most of them would scramble too.

In justice to Dr Gates, it must be rembered that this was written in 1928, when the human race seemed to have some grounds for complacency; she could hardly foresee that another decade would teach us that we are not much better off than Thorndike's cats. There is plenty of food in the world, plenty of everything we need; but mankind has got itself into a complicated set of boxes—psychological and emotional—and does not seem able to find the way through. Some men are patiently trying to think it out; but most of what is going on looks like hit-or-miss floundering, and often a stubborn persistence in what is obviously the wrong way.

I will give the psychologists another illustration of the cat's defects as a reasoner, demanding no payment except the privilege of asking, "So what?" The cats in the New York Aquarium, employed to keep out rats, have been taught not to eat the fish. On arrival they are given electric eels to play with, and after they have had a few shocks they conclude that anything in the Aquarium tanks (or more probably anything with the Aquarium smell) is electrified too. Or, as Mark Twain once summarized it, a cat who has once sat on a hot stove will never thereafter sit on a cold stove.

And the human race? Most of the shoestring speculators of 1929 had resolved by 1932 that they would never fool with the stock market again. Yet a good deal of money has been made in the stock market since 1932. We all despise the people who don't know what we know. My cat has been trained not to catch birds; but each summer when he arrives at his country home he meets a new generation of birds who do not know that he will let them alone. As he lies peacefully under a bush and listens to their frightened shriekings he wears an expression of utter contempt—such contempt as a psychologist might feel for a cat who was slow to find his way through a set of trick boxes.

V

The fact is that ailourology, like anthropology, is a social science; and we have all learned by now that the exact technique of the physical sciences has only a limited application in such fields. Dr Gates indeed appears to suspect this; after her long debunking of the cat she qualifies by quoting Virginia Roderick's conclusion that "there is no answer to most questions about the cat; she has kept herself wrapped in mystery for some three thousand years, and there's no use trying to solve her now." At any rate the insight of the artist will come much nearer a solution than the meticulous experiments of the laboratory scientist. Anyone who knows cats will acknowledge that the one best thing ever written about them, the concentrated quintessence of so much ailourology as we know, is Kipling's *The Cat Who Walked by Himself*. What that cat thought, what any cat thinks as he walks in the wet wild woods by his wild lone, waving his wild tail, no one can surely say. Not just what we should be thinking, certainly—but perhaps something not altogether alien to our ideas and feelings.

That cats experience the simpler emotions—desire, anger, fear, contentment—no one would deny; but they can have more complex emotions too, both good and bad. My cat, given three seconds to get ready, can run any dog out of the yard; but once a dog tearing in at high speed came on him unexpectedly from behind a bush, and General Gray behaved as other veteran troops have behaved in a similar situation. He ran; and being a cat, he ran up a tree. There he halted and collected himself and looked down at that dog; and you could see the shame in his face, the sense of an imperative obligation to retrieve his self-respect. A moment later he came down the tree and chased the dog out of the yard, as usual.

Charles Willis Thompson once lived with a Persian cat named Thomas Jefferson Topaz, and owned a bull-dog named William Howard Woof. The two were great friends and one night they were asleep together in the living room—the bulldog on the rug, the cat precariously extended on the arm of a chair. Too precariously; eventually he fell off, and was painfully awakened when he hit the floor. His reaction, in this humiliating situation, was entirely human; self-respect forbade him to admit that his misfortune was his own fault. He looked around for somebody else to blame it on, and walked over and slapped the slumbering and innocent dog.

Not only the cat's intellectual but his emotional range is a good deal wider than can be measured by laboratory methods. This does not prove that he is a philosopher, but still less can the scientists prove that he is not. He looks philosophic, he behaves philosophically in his own affairs; he can act with speed and power when he needs to but he avoids all waste exertion, all effort that has no purpose *to a cat;* when there is time he weighs his decisions—no cat ever went through a door held open for him without measured pondering of the arguments for and against the step; he does what he wants to in so far as he can, and except in peril of his life wastes no energy on the impossible. What he thinks of human doings no one knows; but we can occasionally make plausible guesses. One of the most engaging tail wavers in literature is Viktor Scheffel's black tom cat Hiddigeigei. Only a character of fiction, to be sure; you may say it is Scheffel, not Hiddigeigei speaking when he concludes some derogatory observations on human behavior:

> *Menschentun ist bloss Verkehrtes,*
> *Menschentun ist Ach und Krach.*
> *Im Bewusstsein seines Wertes*
> *Sitzt der Kater auf dem Dach.*

But so I have seen a Persian cat on the roof watch the guests stumble out from a cocktail party across the road; if his verdict was not the same as Hiddigeigei's, then you can read nothing in a face.

Those who know cats best, at any rate, feel that they have a sort of wisdom denied to us; even if we may also have a sort denied to them—of which, God knows, we show little trace at present. Why let yourself be

kept by a cat? Because there is little human companionship so satisfying as that of a friend of superhuman dignity and poise, who looks wise, behaves wisely in his
own affairs, and regards your tribulations with an
affectionate—and silent—sympathy.

The late Clarence Day once speculated on what the
world would be like if the species that became dominant had been super-cats instead of super-monkeys.
Life would be, he concluded, much more brilliant and
beautiful and exciting. How did it happen that this
noble species fell behind a tribe of feeble chatterers
who in the Tertiary jungles could have been no more
than an inconsiderable nuisance? The cats were too
philosophic, he concluded, and too individualistic; the
simians progressed by their insatiable curiosity and their
capacity for co-operation. But this was written some
twenty or twenty-five years ago; super-simian co-operation is not conspicuous at present, and simian curiosity
has led to the finding out of many inventions, such as
submarines and bombing planes. Cats fight, but for reasons that usually make more sense than ours; and they
stop fighting when they have settled the point immediately at issue; they have not risen to the concept of
totalitarian war. They may yet get a chance to see what
they can make of the world; unless, as Harlow Shapley
once suggested, we simians leave our planet in such condition that it will be a fit inheritance for no species but
the cockroach.

The Imperfect Wagnerite

THE IMPERFECT WAGNERITE

NOW that the Metropolitan Opera Company has survived another crisis, some of us veteran opera goers can sit back thankfully and reflect on what we should have missed if it had gone the way of other adornments of the fat years. I do not claim to speak for the "opera public"; the New York opera, at least, has several publics. But I am a specimen of perhaps the most truly devoted public of them all—the people who go to the opera house, buying seats when they can afford it and standing up when times are hard, for no social or racial or customary reason, but simply because we like opera. Of course we could hear opera even if the Metropolitan closed; there are minor-league companies that give you a pretty good show for a very moderate amount of money. If you prefer a passably good performance of a good opera to a first-rate performance of a dull opera (and if you do not, you are no true opera fan) those companies can slake your thirst for Italian and French opera, for *Tannhäuser* and even for *Lohengrin*. But in one respect the Metropolitan, to us middle-aged middle-class citizens who go to the opera only because we like it, is irreplaceable—only there, regularly every season, can you hear *The Ring;* and as we grow older, *The Ring* seems more and more the one indispensable item of the operatic repertoire.

What about *Tristan?* says the lady in the back row. Madam, you can have *Tristan;* an hour of it, any hour, is a good show; but four hours of *Tristan* is a great deal of the same thing. *Tristan* is about love, but *The Ring* is about something which cannot be described by any term less comprehensive than Life; and on that topic it offers an all too pertinent commentary. When it no longer has anything to say to the spectator that will be a sign that the present human race has turned into something else, better or worse. So long as there are men of our kind, men who can imagine and desire more than they can accomplish, you are lucky if you can come away from the full cycle of *The Ring* without saying to yourself, *"De te fabula narratur."*

But what the devil does it mean, then? says the embittered boxholder who has to appear regularly at the opera house for the sake of his social position, but has never been able to understand what anybody could see in this myth of gods and giants, dwarfs and heroes, with its interminable monologues and wearisome repetitions. Forget the myth, brother, and all the hoyotoho and wagalaweia; *"The Ring* is a drama of today, not of a remote and fabulous antiquity." So wrote, some forty years ago, a London music critic who had also written some plays which were beginning to get productions; his name was George Bernard Shaw. It is still a drama of today, and of every day until the impulse that began with the Renaissance either gets somewhere or finally gutters out. Shaw's interpretation (in *The Perfect Wagnerite*) treats *The Ring* not only as a brief in the case of The Spirit *vs*. The Letter, which it is as surely as are the epistles of St Paul, but also as a parable of the revolution of 1848, in which Wagner was disastrously involved. Before the revolution, when he was conductor at the Dresden Opera House, he had projected a music drama called *The Death of Siegfried;* after he lost his job and had to escape to Switzerland to save his life he expanded this into a series of four music dramas which turned out to be less about Siegfried than about Wotan. Shaw equates Wotan with the well-intentioned ruler, temporal or spiritual, who must rule by law yet finds his own evolving best intention (personified in Brünnhilde) outgrowing the law. Fricka is the Spirit of the Constitution, Alberich the sort of early industrialist depicted in Marx's *Capital,* Fafner the coupon clipper, and so on. Wotan is unable to realize his good intentions; but the gods (like modern man) can imagine and try to create a nobler species than themselves, the Heroes. So the world is saved at last by Siegfried, the

Uninhibited Natural Man who lives wholly by his unconscious, yet finds that in harmony with his best conscious desire.

Whether Shaw would still stand by that interpretation,
written in 1898, I do not know. We have learned rather
more than was then known about the Uninhibited Natural Man, and the drives of his unconscious no longer
seem the surest foundation on which to build the perfect
society. Even in 1898 there was one great stumbling-
block in the way of Shaw's exegesis—*Götterdämmerung*.
(This time-honored title seems preferable to any English
equivalent.) Siegfried did not triumph; enmeshed in
the ancestral curse, he failed, and his death involved
the end of the old gods who had created him and the
clearing of the ground for a new order in which neither
gods nor heroes would have any part—perhaps a dictatorship of the proletariat which had served the Gibichungs, or of some future Hagen who might seize
power in their name. Bring the Shavian parable up to
date, with Siegfried as Hitler, and it may be a preview
of the history of the next few decades.

So far the parallel has been uncannily exact, except
that the spectators can see no particular reason to prefer
Siegfried to Hagen. In September 1939, when we heard
the bands playing a march built around the Siegfried
Motive as Hitler made his triumphal entry into Danzig,
many of us remembered September 1938, when the

sword that Siegfried had forged was brandished in the air, and Wotan's umbrella fell to pieces before the mere wind of its whirling. (The old gentleman has since got himself a new weapon, which may perhaps be more effective; but the treaties and pledges engraved on the shaft of the old one have flown into illegible splinters.) Possibly the parallel will persist to the end, now that an ex-champagne salesman has mixed the Hero a magic drink which made him forget his old loves (ideas, not women); but at this writing we are no farther along than the first act of *Götterdämmerung,* and maybe Dr Goebbels has rewritten the plot. All we can be sure of is that Hitler makes a better Siegfried than Siegfried himself ever did; he knows what to do with the ring.

None of this could have been foreseen when *The Perfect Wagnerite* was written; but Shaw got around *Götterdämmerung* very ingeniously on historical grounds. Last of the operas in the cycle, it was written first; Wagner had sketched it, out of old mythological materials, before the unsuccessful revolution of 1848. After the revolution, discovering that it needed prefatory explanation, he wrote the other three operas of the cycle in reverse order, filling them with the ideas that were most on his mind at the time. It was years, however, before production of *The Ring* was possible; Wagner put off finishing the music, and when at last he got around to it in the early seventies he must have realized that *Götterdämmerung* did not fit into his great musical-dramatic parable of the revolution at all. Logically the drama ends when Siegfried shatters Wotan's spear, and goes on through the fire to awaken Brünnhilde.

By the early seventies times had changed; Bismarck had triumphed, the Paris Commune had failed; Wagner was dependent on a king's favor and pretty much disillusioned with revolutionaries. "Alberich had got the ring back and was marrying into the best Walhall families," and respectability had humanized him; he was more like Krupp or Carnegie than like the early manufacturers described by Marx and Engels. Wagner realized that between Siegmund who failed and Siegfried who triumphed several generations must intervene; and since it would have been an impossible task to rewrite his whole tetralogy, he let *Götterdämmerung* go as written, counting on the "enormously elaborate and gorgeous musical fabric" to make the listener forget the logical irrelevance.

II

For the nineties, this interpretation was plausible enough; but we know more now about the fruits of Wagner's doctrines, and about the seeds from which they sprang. Wagner's politics and "metapolitics" (as one of his correspondents called them) are subjected to a more searching, and startling, analysis than Shaw ever gave them by Peter Viereck, in *Common Sense* for November and December 1939. Mr Viereck, who has read far more deeply in Wagner's political writings than I— or apparently than Shaw—says that Wagner was "the most important single fountain-head of Nazi ideology"; which trickled down through Houston Stewart Chamberlain, Alfred Rosenberg, and Dietrich Eckart to a man who could make it work.

The filiation, as Viereck cites it, is striking and convincing; and perhaps the motivation too. Wagner in Paris in the early forties, poor, unsuccessful and unknown, felt "homeless," as did Hitler later in Vienna; he longed (Viereck's phrasing) "to become an organic part of a greater unity"—no trivial part, we may be sure. Of the varieties of Nazi doctrine, the one closest to his views seems to have been the Nazism of Roehm and Gregor Strasser; in 1848 Wagner wanted "a political army of the masses"—just what Roehm wanted in 1934, an ambition that led to his liquidation; and even after 1871, says Peter Viereck, he was still the enemy of property. (Like Shaw he could afford to be, having by that time as much property as he needed.) It is curious that these views, once heresy, seem to be quite orthodox now; Germany has a mass army, far more politicalized than it was two years ago, and property has been pretty thoroughly subjected to the use of the state. But note that they did not become orthodox till the men who might once have climbed to the top with the aid of these doctrines had been put out of the way.

In other respects Wagner's ideas differed greatly from their modern development. He was, says Viereck, no imperialist or militarist; he wanted Germany to be supreme, but in art and thought; the "revolt of instinct against legalism and reason" which, in varying forms, is the basic theme of *The Ring* had in mind more admirable instincts than those that find vent in, for instance, the treatment of prisoners in Dachau. The "uncomposed passage" near the very end of the *Götterdämmerung* libretto which, in Wagner's opinion, was a summary of the whole tetralogy set Love as the highest good; and it may not have occurred to Wagner that the whole argument for legalism is that when you take off the curbs on instinct you let loose not merely the praiseworthy instincts, but whatever instincts there are.

All of which suggests that *The Ring* is all things to all men. Shaw, out of doctrines potentially more explosive than Wagner himself perhaps ever realized, drew what was congenial to Shaw, and to the enlightened drawing-room gradualism of the nineties which liked to believe, over the teacups, that it was revolutionary. But presently there came along an artist greater than Shaw— an unsuccessful artist as yet, because he had been working in the wrong medium—who, like Shaw, took from Wagner what he could appreciate; and by the power of his warped genius transmuted it into something very different, and far more formidable.

Wagner might have been thoroughly scandalized if he had seen what he helped to bring into being—at least the Wagner who wrote *The Rhine Gold* and *The Valkyrie,* the Wagner who was primarily interested in Wotan. For Wotan had a conscience; like Bethmann-Hollweg, he was capable of recognizing and admitting that he had done wrong, even if he found it expedient to keep the profits. Wotan would have been ashamed of the Nazis; and so perhaps would his creator.

But Siegfried is something else; and so must have been the Wagner who was capable of creating Siegfried. To Siegfried such concepts as Right and Wrong had no meaning; his universe was divided into What I Want, and What I Don't Happen to Want, Yet. There were periods in Wagner's life when he seemed to have the same attitude, at least as regarded money and women; certainly the man who created Siegfried, perhaps without fully realizing what he was creating, had some appalling potentialities which were left for other men to realize.

Siegfried, says Viereck, is "the incarnation of the *Führerprinzip;* in his role as individual he is a mere atomistic mortal, as personification of the German *Volk* he shares its divinity." True, so far as it goes; but the Siegfried that Wagner created out of the much simpler figure of medieval legend is far more than that; he is the incarnation of the Nazi character as we have seen it displayed in action. And here is the mystery. How could even such an artist as Wagner prefigure, with such amazing accuracy, a type-character which was not to come into existence for nearly three quarters of a century?

Among the Germans he knew, conservatives or revolutionaries, there was nobody at all like Siegfried (except perhaps Richard Wagner, or one of the aspects of Richard Wagner that seldom came to the surface) ; yet in our day, before our eyes, Siegfried has come to life by the million. Was this prophetic intuition such as no other artist has ever displayed? Or—I am rationalist enough to be ashamed of suggesting this, yet it seems a possibility that must be mentioned—was Siegfried always latent in the soul of the German people, and Wagner only the inspired medium who succeeded in materializing him? Or—a more congenial and three-dimensional interpretation—has a considerable part of the German people been formed in the image of Siegfried by long and zealous attendance at the opera house? I leave these questions to the race-psychologists, without promising much confidence in their answer, whatever it may be. *Felix qui potuit rerum cognoscere causas.*

III

So much for the history of Wotan and of Siegfried as political parable and political inspiration. But *The Ring* is spacious enough to admit of more than one interpretation, and what was in the mind of such an artist as Wagner when he wrote it is perhaps not altogether to be grasped even by such a mind as Shaw's. I do not pretend to get more out of it than Shaw got; but I get something different, which no less than Shaw's interpretation may have been implicit in Wagner's vision.

Who cares, you may ask, what I think it means or what Shaw thinks it means? The question is what Wagner thought it means. Unfortunately Wagner has told us what he thought, and Shaw has proved out of his own mouth that he was wrong. Reading Schopenhauer's *Die Welt als Wille und Vorstellung* after he had finished the libretto of *The Ring*, Wagner felt in his first enthusiasm that here was a logical exposition of the very ideas he had set forth in poetry; "now at last," he wrote, "I understand my Wotan." In some respects—emphasis on the superiority of the unconscious to Reason, for instance—Wagner's philosophy does indeed resemble Schopenhauer's; but in the Wotan of *The Rhine Gold* and *The Valkyrie* there is none of Schopenhauer's negation and resignation. He was always in there trying;

only when he was old and tired and beaten did he become a disciple of Schopenhauer.*

So never mind what Wagner thought he had written; it is an old story (most recently exemplified by the autobiography of H. G. Wells) that a first-rate writer may not know what he is really doing. It is also an old story that what you get out of a work of art is largely determined by what you bring to it; the spectator of *The Ring,* says Shaw, will recognize in it "an image of the life he is himself fighting his way through." If he is trying to save the world, as was Shaw in the nineties, or to rule the world, as are other men today, he will read into it a parable of the world revolution; and he can equally see his own problems reflected in it if he is trying to do no more than show some creditable result for his life's work, and make of himself as decent a figure as the wear and tear of living will permit.

---

* Wagner seems to have been as misleading in this citation of his sources as he was in his notion of what he meant. "The idea of spiritual consummation and appeasement through a mystical Death-in-Love was in Wagner's mind, and is to be found in his writings, before he had even heard of Schopenhauer," says Lawrence Gilman (*Wagner's Operas,* p. 156). "It was scarcely necessary for him to give credit to Schopenhauer for ideas which had already come to him from the source which had been drawn upon by them both—those philosophical speculations of ancient India, into which the poet-composer had penetrated so much more deeply and intuitively than the philosopher."

If you are only an imperfect Wagnerite, a middle-aged middle-class citizen who goes to the opera because he likes it, you can read in the history of Wotan (*Götterdämmerung* included) the greatest apologue ever written of the life of the Average Man. Or if this seems disrespectful to Wotan, call him the typical Rather-Better-Than-Average Man; the man whose ambitions, by no means wholly unselfish, still aim at socially useful ends; who catches a vision of good things that he hopes to accomplish, and then finds himself in middle age impotent to accomplish them, paralyzed by his innate shortcomings and by the ineluctable consequences of his own mistakes.

IV

Wotan's troubles, like those of most young married men, began when he became a home owner. Up to that time he had apparently done pretty well; when we first see him he is the executive of a considerable organization, he has made some advantageous contracts, and he is successful enough to enlist the services of a smart lawyer, Loge, who can be depended on to find a loophole in any contract that may prove inconvenient. Wotan also has a wife, Fricka, whom he had wanted badly enough before he got her (or so he says) to have given his only remaining eye for her. (He had spent the other one for his education.)

Nevertheless, there are already signs of tension between husband and wife. "I like women too well to suit you," he confesses; but as yet other women are no problem in themselves; they are only the symptom of a restlessness in Wotan, an itch for variety, that Fricka cannot share. So, agreeing with Herbert Hoover that nobody ever sang "Home, Sweet Home" to a bundle of rent receipts, she has fallen in with Wotan's project of acquiring a suburban home, in the hope that her husband will be so proud of his establishment that he will stay at home in the evening. (Plenty of apartment wives will recognize her feelings.) So badly does she want the house that she is not much worried about the price; her husband is doing well in the world; he has assured her that they can afford it; with the self-confidence of a rising young executive he has left her out of the negotiations with the contractors—and now she and her husband suddenly discover that the new home will cost more than they can pay.

Wotan gets out of this difficulty more luckily than the average young man—thanks to his lawyer. Usually such talent as Loge's serves the title company; with his professional skill backing up Fafner's brutal violence, the home owner goes into peonage for the rest of his life. But Wotan pays for his house only by letting himself in for something even more inconvenient than mortgages; he raises the money by the first unmistakably crooked deal of his life, behaving so badly that even his lawyer is ashamed of him. Wotan has overcome his moral scruples, Shaw points out, by working up a moral fervor over the misuse Alberich would have made of the money which Wotan intends to employ for worthy purposes; but presently he meets a woman (a widow with three children, older, more experienced, and wiser than his wife) who recalls him to reality. He has behaved badly because it seemed at the moment that it was the only way out; and thereby he has started a chain of consequences whose end is far beyond his seeing. Always after that he must worry, and be a little afraid.

For the moment Wotan has triumphed, and triumphed very splendidly as the rainbow bridge leaps across the chasm, and the gods cross over it to Walhall on the distant heights. . . . What was once the music of the future is already, to a good many people, the music of the past; and it may be that no one can be deeply moved by it who did not get his emotional set before the nineteenth century went out. But there is an emotion that most men are lucky enough to experience at least once or twice in their lives, an emotion without which no man's life is complete: the feeling of now-at-last-I'm-beginning-to-get-somewhere. The sudden startling glimpse of a rainbow brilliance as some long-sought objective that has cost work and worry, anxiety and apprehension and self-denial and pain, is at last attained—the triumphal culmination of a long struggle, opening the way (so it seems in that exalted moment) to even greater triumphs beyond. These words are pitiably inadequate; no words that I have ever seen in print are adequate to describe this particular feeling. Once and only once, to my perhaps archaic taste, it has been expressed adequately—by the rainbow music at the end of *The Rhine Gold*. . . . Yet presently, interwoven with that music, you begin to hear other themes—reminders of what the triumph has cost, of the hidden forces, irrational and incalculable, that have been aroused. Wotan has done something wrong and he knows it; he keeps up his front, but precisely because he is a fairly decent god, as gods go, he never quite gets over it.

Nor is the stirring up of hatred, the unleashing of a curse, the only cost of Walhall; something irreparable has happened to Wotan's relation to his wife. Before this real-estate transaction she may have worried about his restlessness, but she respected him; he might be just a big grown-up boy in some ways, but nobody could deny his business ability. Now Fricka has to recognize that her husband made a fool of himself, that only Loge, whom she despises, saved the family from disaster. Moreover, a marital harmony that had survived ordinary stresses cracked wide open in a money crisis; husband and wife under pressure displayed unsuspected motivations, utterly irreconcilable standards of value; everything each of them did got on the other's nerves, they lost their tempers and blurted out unpleasant truths that can never be forgotten. The quarrel is over, they move into Walhall; but an indispensable illusion has been shattered, Fricka can no longer respect or trust her husband. . . . While Wotan, recalling how maddeningly his wife nagged him when he was worrying his head off about money, finds his thoughts going back to that widow he lately met, and her refreshingly realistic point of view. It could do no harm to look her up again—with no sentimental intentions, of course; his interest in Erda is purely intellectual. . . .

You can read in *The Rhine Gold,* says Shaw, the whole tragedy of human history; and you can also read in it such a tragi-comedy as is played out a dozen times a year in every commuting suburb. There stands the House, acquired at such a cost, and not in money alone; still it is a good house, and the young people have taken title and moved in, even though the mortgage hangs heavy over their heads; the quarrel that broke out during the negotiations with the title company has been made up, and now they are going to live happily ever after.

But nothing will ever be quite the same again.

V

The Valkyrie shows us Wotan and Fricka in middle age, successful, prosperous, and miserable. Wotan has continued to do amazingly well for himself, but always there hangs over him the tormenting realization that this may not last, that something he did years ago because it seemed best at the time, without ever foreseeing its consequences, may ultimately ruin him. And there is nothing he can do about it; tied down with promises and commitments, he cannot remove the peril without wrecking the whole social fabric of which he is a part.

As for his domestic relations, he and Fricka maintain the dignified front of a successful middle-aged married couple, but the true situation is plain enough to anybody who knows them well; Brünnhilde, at the beginning of the second act, hurriedly leaves Wotan with the cheerful observation (I translate freely): "You're going to catch hell; here comes your wife." Brünnhilde did not then know of anything particular and recent that Wotan had done to catch hell about, but she knew Fricka, and Wotan too. He still has that itch for variety, yet he has always treated his wife with proper respect; she has a remarkably fine car (which the limitations of stage production seldom permit the audience to see); over certain fields of their common interest she is supreme; her husband seems to have done about everything for her that a man can do for his wife, except be faithful to her. . . . That widow now, Erda—he had gone to see her, drawn by a purely intellectual attraction; he wanted to ask her some questions. But apparently she was lonesome, she did not want to talk about abstract topics; and it occurred to Wotan that a man and a woman cannot be sure that they are intellectually congenial till they have got more urgent matters off their minds. This seems to have been his first affair, and no doubt he got into it without ever exactly intending to; but there were others. . . . And others. . . .

The painful scene between Wotan and Fricka in the second act has a bisexual application that could hardly have been dreamed of in Wagner's day, when only women of the aristocracy had much freedom; nowadays there are wives as well as husbands who could play Wotan's part, husbands as well as wives who could play Fricka's. The tragedy is Wotan's, and Fricka has an extremely unsympathetic part; yet Wagner as an artist could not help letting us see the psychological springs and explanation of her behavior; she was so rigorously insistent on maintaining the outward front of marriage, even if nothing but hatred was behind it, because her own marriage had ceased to be anything but front. She had to cling to the one thing she had left. It may be that when Wagner wrote her lines he was thinking of the Spirit of Constitutional Law; but it may be also that he was thinking of a woman named Minna Planer Wagner, so uncharitably suspicious of her husband's purely intellectual interest in other women. (Yet this same Minna had once been the gay mistress who so delighted him, the young bride with whom he planned their private Walhall. . . .)

Fricka demanded that Wotan must surrender to her

vengeance what he loved best—his son Siegmund, be-
gotten to accomplish what Wotan could not do himself;
and Wotan, who had begun by telling himself valor-
ously, "I've got to stand up to her," discovered that he
could not stand up to her because she had too much on
him. What would become of him if contracts were disregarded? Besides, he does not come into court with
clean hands. Siegmund has run off with another man's
wife; no wonder, says Fricka, that you stand up for him,
you who are always running around with other women.
She says enough to let Wotan see that she could easily
say more if necessary; so Siegmund must die, not so much
because of what he did as because of what his father did
before he was ever born.

You need not read any Shavian allegory of education
and eugenics into the relation between Wotan and Siegmund. Every man believes, for a while, that he is creating a nobler race to replace himself; that his children
will accomplish, by and large, what he himself had intended before he got involved. And I know of no more
bitter experience in the life of the average man (or
average woman) than the slow realization that your
children who once seemed beings of another order,
brighter and freer and better, must grow up to become
members of the human race; that instead of realizing all
the things on which you have somehow missed, they
must make their mistakes, meet with their irreparable

disappointments, see themselves enmeshed in the consequences of their own well-intentioned blunders—precisely like their grandparents' children, and everybody
else's children since time began. Not always is the responsibility for their misfortunes so clear as in Siegmund's case; but any conscientious parent must feel
some qualms when he sees his children getting into
trouble, ultimately, because they inherited from their
parents their share of human frailty.

But Wotan's expiation does not end with the failures
of his son. When Brünnhilde, who embodies Wotan's
best intention, saves what she can from the disaster,
Wotan has to punish her—suppress his own best intention, do something that he knows is wrong, because in
the past he has done things that turned out to be wrong,
though he never suspected it at the time. A man in
that position is about as far down as he can ever get.
Maybe you think Wotan deserved it; but not many men,
even if they never cheated anybody out of any money and
are unfailingly loyal to their wives, can survey their
records from middle age without perceiving something
that had seemed the best thing to do at the time, but
turned out to be disastrous. Wotan is a tragic figure
precisely because he is the Average Fairly Decent Man,
who generally tries to do the best he can and eventually
finds himself entangled in unforeseen consequences.
Now he is helpless; he must do what is expected of him,

keep up a front. In *The Rhine Gold* he swaggers and blusters and keeps up a front from pride, the pride of the young executive who refuses to admit that he has blundered; but in *The Valkyrie* he sacrifices everything to keeping up a front because he knows how much relies on that front for shelter. He is a man with dependents now—all the gods must fall if Wotan falls; the head of a family, the keystone of a widespread organization. How faulty that organization is he realizes better than anybody else; still he must defend it at any cost, because he cannot think of a practicable alternative that would be any better.

So Wotan, who had once done what seemed best, now does what he has to do, however bad it seems. After he leaves Brünnhilde, Wagner once wrote, the best he can do is to let things take their course. Most men, and most women, sooner or later come to that. Read *The Valkyrie* as anything you like—a parable of nineteenth-century revolution, or of Roosevelt *vs.* the Supreme Court if you prefer; but the man who can sit through it without uncomfortable stirrings of his private conscience is either a paragon of virtue and wisdom or an insufferably complacent fool.

VI

Here, logically, the story of Wotan ends. But Wotan, like most of us, does not end when his existence ceases to have any logical or dramatic justification; he has to go on living. Mr. Thornton Wilder wrote in *The Bridge of San Luis Rey* an excellent story of five people who had the good luck to die at exactly the right time, when they either had just accomplished or seemed just about to accomplish the height of their ambition. Another good story could be written about the people who had the ill fortune to reach the bridge just before, or just after, it fell; who were spared to get across the river, and to discover that there was pretty much the same sort of landscape on the other side.* In almost every man's life there is a moment when he might die with fitness and dignity, with the effect of a good dramatic conclusion; when (like Lincoln) he has just won some great triumph, so that people look helplessly at one another and say, "What shall we do without him?" Or when he stands visibly on the threshold of achievement, so that people shake their heads and say, "What a loss! He was a man who would have gone far." But it is the lot of most of us to linger on until our obituaries provoke some such comment as "What, that old fossil? I thought he'd been dead for years."

Wotan survived himself; in *Siegfried* he is nothing but

---

* I have indeed tried to write it myself—"Man of Destiny," in *Collier's* for March 7, 1936, if anybody cares to look it up. A pretty good story, but the idea still has possibilities not fully explored.

an old fossil, yet he has to go on living till someone is competent to take his place. Like a good many elderly gentlemen of means, he spends his time in travel; he is observant, he picks up a good deal of information, he can answer all the questions anybody asks him and ask questions that less traveled persons are unable to answer; but he cannot do anything about it. He stands by and watches other people striving for what they want, what he wanted once himself; but he is through with striving; things are taking their course, and he has to take their course too. And his wife? We hear no more about her. No doubt, on the rare occasions when Wotan is at home, they get along well enough by keeping out of each other's way; by now they must be too old and tired for either love or hatred.

Yet Wotan has one or two last flickers of energy. He goes to call on Erda for old times' sake, and finds that that once lovely mistress also has grown old and tired, and is disinclined to conversation. ("Good heavens, did the man ever think that what I wanted was to talk to him?") And he meets Siegfried, his grandson who is growing up now, and is about ready to take over the family business; to whom Wotan naturally offers some grandfatherly advice. But Siegfried has no appetite for advice, or for information that might be useful in his business; what he does not know already is not knowledge, and be damned to this old windbag who wants him to stop and talk when he is on his way to see a girl. Whereupon Wotan loses his temper, and feels as a million grandfathers have felt in his place. "What, shall this young squirt, etc.? Not while I can stop him!" But the spear that once ruled the world falls to pieces under Siegfried's sword; its shaft has rotted with time, the contracts so carefully inscribed in it are ancient and forgotten history; the future belongs to a new generation which Wotan, upon acquaintance, does not admire quite so highly as he did when it was still in infancy and could be the repository of all his own unfulfilled aspirations.

Which brings us to Siegfried.

VII

A competent social psychologist might have deduced the whole history of modern Germany, from Bismarck down to Hitler, from this one fact: the Germans are the kind of people who admire such a hero as Siegfried. (Not all of them, to be sure; but a sufficient majority.) *

---

* Truer than I realized when I wrote it. No nation likes to lose a war; but other nations, when they have lost one, eventually manage to reconcile themselves to the plain fact that they were licked, whatever knavish tricks of their enemies they may blame for the disaster. Only Germany must proclaim the dogma, not to be denied except under penalty of excommunication from the *Volksgemeinschaft,* that unbeaten armies were treasonably

Yet for what Siegfried was, no less than for what his father Siegmund was, Wotan was responsible. He had educated Siegmund very carefully; a rigorous education ("my son is not going to be pampered and spoiled, as I was at his age") but one well calculated to fit him for the profession of hero to which his father had destined him. Unfortunately it turned out that education was not enough to guarantee success; Siegmund never had any luck. Yet he stood up against all adversity with a Calvinistic fortitude; he was a man worth fifty of his son. And while he broke up a home (which needed it) he was no promiscuous amorist. Consider his dialogue with Brünnhilde, who has come to invite him to Walhall, and recites its varied attractions. Are there any women in Walhall? asks Siegmund. Why, yes, says Brünnhilde; we girls are there. But, says Siegmund, can I bring my wife? And upon learning that he cannot—Give my regards to Walhall, he tells her; I'm not coming. The result of this conversation, curiously enough, is to inspire Brünnhilde with an overpowering devotion not only to Siegmund but to his wife; but then Brünnhilde is still a goddess, not yet a woman.

But if Siegmund's education made a man, it did not

betrayed by Jews and democrats within—because three generations of Germans have been conditioned by the Ring operas to the conviction that the German Hero can never be struck down except by a stab in the back.

make a successful man; so Wotan lost his faith in education and let Siegfried grow up anyhow, with consequences which are a good advertisement for a formal schooling. "Having had no god to instruct him in the art of unhappiness," says Shaw, "Siegfried inherits none of his father's ill luck"; but that is a nineteenth-century judgment which Shaw might repudiate today. Siegfried has plenty of ill luck in *Götterdämmerung;* if he had been better educated he might have learned that there are influences which make a man forget what he ought to remember. Cocky, arrogant, bumptious, he grew up not only without inhibitions, but without manners and without knowledge. It is true that a remarkable woman fell in love with him, but he was the only man in sight at the time; a good many superior women have married the men they did for no better reason.

If the young Siegfried is disagreeable, Siegfried in middle age is intolerable. So far luck has been with him, everything he tried has come off, so naturally he thinks he knows it all. After a while he gets bored with country life on Brünnhilde's rock and goes back to town to achieve some more achievements; he is supposed to have learned all that his wife could teach him, but he must have been a dull pupil, for the very first thing he does is to stumble into a clip joint. (The hall of the Gibichungs deserves no politer description, considering what happened to Siegfried there.) Yet it is impossible to be sorry for him when you see how he behaves in the last act of *Götterdämmerung*.

Siegfried, who has got rid of Brünnhilde and married again, is on his way to meet his brothers-in-law when he encounters three girls, and pauses for what he probably considers a little airy repartee. He keeps up his snappy come-backs till they ask him for his ring; and he can think of no better reason for not giving it to them than that his wife might not like it. (Why drag her in?) Then he tells them, at some length, what a remarkable man he is; and when they lose interest in the conversation and walk out on him he says to himself (not the ideal listener, but better than none) that he knows all about women, and would certainly have dated up one of those girls if he were not a respectable married man.

Then he meets his brothers-in-law, and they have a few drinks; and our hero consents to tell them some stories— about himself of course. He talks on and on, till one of the others suggests that they had better have another drink. They have it, and then Siegfried starts right in again—this time, about his prowess with women; at which point one of the listeners loses his patience and reaches for his spear. . . . Breathes there the man with soul so dead that he has not sometimes wanted to do, to some interminable autobiographer at the luncheon table, exactly what Hagen did to Siegfried?

Meanwhile we have heard one last report about

Wotan; he is sitting in Walhall amid the cordwood into which he has chopped the World Ash Tree from which he once drew his power, and waiting. This, says Shaw contemptuously, belongs to the old legendary materials with which Wagner began *The Ring*. Old, Mr Shaw? Legendary, Mr Shaw? More than almost anything else in the tetralogy, that is a story of today and of every day; it may not fit into the Shavian parable of the revolution that never came off, but it fits with appalling exactitude into the story of the Average Man. For unless he meets with what is ironically termed an untimely end, this is what the Average Man must come to at last—an old, weary, forgotten figure, sitting amid the debris of everything that he once cared about; waiting, with an apathy that does not deserve to be called patience, for an exit that might have been made with greater dignity long before. This is the end of all the striving, good and bad—all the struggles and all the visions, all the triumphs and all the mistakes; all the posturings and boastings, all the hatred and malice and all the love and forbearance too. The normal end of man.

VIII

It is not a very pleasing prospect; and the endeavor to get us somehow reconciled to it has evoked some of the most brilliant flights of human genius. One such is the fifteenth chapter of First Corinthians, another the finale of *Götterdämmerung*. Some people's psychic receiving sets are attuned to the one, some to the other; personally I prefer *Götterdämmerung,* even though no earthly theater can ever produce that last scene quite as Wagner conceived it.*

Wagner tells you, as St Paul tells you, that the immediate tragedy does not really matter; it is part of a Whole, and the Whole is all right. So much of the Whole as we can see at present (not very much, to be sure) offers little evidence in support of that contention; you must be convinced, if you are convinced at all, in some new dimension, on some plane beyond the reach of mere human reason. Wagner transcends reason with music, St Paul transcends it by faith; but Paul uses words, and combines those words into intelligible ideas, so reason cannot help getting hold of his argument and finding it lacking in cogency. So long as Wagner sticks to words he too is unconvincing; but in the last five minutes he lets the orchestra do his talking, and no man can pick flaws in that argument. Perhaps all he gives you is a species of intoxication; when you have come out from under the spell, when you have left the opera house and

---

* Except perhaps the Radio City Music Hall, built subsequently to this writing. I hope to live to see the day when the Metropolitan Opera Company will move over to the Music Hall for its spring cycle of the Ring operas.

gone down into the subway (or into your limousine, if that is where you go) you find yourself back again in a world where the Whole is no greater than the sum of its parts; and a good many of those parts are hard to fit into any totality that makes sense. Perhaps you have only been hearing some music, after all. . . .

Only hearing some music—but what music! Old-fashioned music, it may be; but on the pre-war generations it still has its unequaled effect. The artist has created his own world, and what he says is valid within its dimensions, whether it squares with logic or not. Alberich's curse is as good an explanation as the temptation of Eve for the fact, obvious to anyone who has been around for any length of time, that there is some perhaps incurable inadequacy in men and women, which is likely to bring their best intentions to nothing or worse than nothing; yet we like to feel, even if we cannot quite bring ourselves to believe, that some day, somehow, that failing will be corrected. To enable some of us to feel that for the moment, even if we can no longer feel it when we have come out on the street, the finale of *Götterdämmerung* is more powerful than the assurance that Death is swallowed up in Victory. If the Average Man, at the end of his days, cannot congratulate himself on any particularly impressive achievement, it may give him some solace to reflect that one of his kind, once upon a time, evoked from a great artist the noblest of elegies.

On Not Being Dead, As Reported

ON NOT BEING DEAD, AS REPORTED

WICE it has been my fortune to be reported missing in a catastrophe, and probably dead. Each
time I denied the story as soon as I heard it, and seem to
have been more generally believed than is usually the
case when people have to contradict something that the
papers have said about them; but if it happens again I
shall fall back on that favorite formula of those whose
misdeeds are unexpectedly brought to light, and refuse
to dignify the rumor with a denial. For a third denial
might not be wholly convincing, even to me; where
there is smoke there is generally some fire; such an oc-
currence is bound to set you wondering if there may not
be some truth in the story after all. And beyond that, to
turn up alive after you have been reported dead is an un-
warrantable imposition on your friends.

The first time it happened I was only twenty-six, and
my repudiation of the canard was accordingly convinced
and vigorous. I happened to be crossing from Holland
to England on a steamer that was submarined and sunk—
one of the most placid submarine sinkings on record, for

the British Navy had time to get not only all the passengers but all their baggage off before she went under. (Indeed, the ship herself was raised after the war and put back into service, and there she is to this day, all ready to be sunk again.) But cross-channel communication was slow and uncertain in 1916; all that was known at first was that the ship had been sunk. Nothing had been heard about the passengers, so the Dutch public leaped to the conclusion which in those days was usually correct; and some days passed before my friends, and enemies, in Holland learned that I had not gone to the bottom after all.

My friends, I am afraid, took it in their stride; even before America was in the war anybody with an international acquaintance had become hardened to hearing the unexpected news of some friend's violent death any morning. When so many good men were being killed at the front every day there was no reason to waste any particular grief on a neutral who had accidentally got in the way of the war and been run over. The effect on my enemies was, in the long run, more deplorable.

They were not my enemies really—only a group of high-minded people who held with great fervor ideals on whose practicability I had been compelled to throw some doubt, in print; they were in fact the leaders and delegates of the Ford Peace Party, and they looked on me as one unsaved, who had not seen the light. Very likely there was more in that view than I would admit at the time. I still think the Ford Peace Party was a crazy enterprise; but an endeavor, however visionary and inadequate, to stop a war that was wrecking Europe appears in retrospect a little less crazy than most of the other purposes that were prevalent in Europe in 1916.

However, I was unable to see eye to eye with the leaders of this Children's Crusade, so it had sometimes come to black looks and harsh words. But when I was reported dead those who had thought so poorly of me were engulfed in a wave of Christian charity. "What a pity!" they said. "He was a young man of great promise." It was some years before I realized how callously inconsiderate it had been for me to turn up after that, alive and well, and just as unsaved as ever. Nobody who has risen to a noble gesture of generosity and forgiveness likes to be made to look foolish a couple of days later.

II

My alleged decease got no newspaper publicity that time, at least not in any newspaper that found me worthy of extended mention; so there was no opportunity to enjoy what might seem to the unthinking the rare privilege of reading my own obituary. But I know men who have had that privilege, and they tell me it is anything but a pleasure.

You may be scandalized at the discovery that the papers thought you were worth no more than a paragraph or two when you would have supposed you rated at least half a column. Even if you get as much (or almost as much) space as you think you deserve, you are likely to find that the source material which the writer of the obituary discovered in the clippings in the newspaper morgue deals chiefly with what you had always regarded as trivial aspects of your career; or probably indeed with its scandalous aspects, if it has had any. This is natural; all the writer has found is some record of the occasions on which you said or did something that was news; and all of us except the great are most likely to become news by being conspicuously wicked, conspicuously unfortunate, or conspicuously ridiculous. Long years of industry and success in the hardware business, a lifetime of zealous and fruitful service to the church or the lodge, will pass all but unnoticed by the press. Whereas there are likely to be columns and columns in the newspaper files about the unfortunate occasion when that unbalanced woman to whom you had foolishly lent money, for no reason at all except disinterested benevolence, sued you for breach of promise, claiming that she never knew you were married.

For when a man dies the newspaper is compelled to function, to the best of its ability, as the Voice of History. Conscious enough of its own inadequacy, it must nevertheless do the best it can to represent the man not as he seemed to himself or to those who loved him (nor to those who hated him either) ; but the man as he was objectively, against his background, in proportion to his universe. How often when I was a young reporter have I called up a bereaved family for information about the deceased, to be told that he was one of Nature's noblemen and the kindest husband and father that ever lived. It takes a certain amount of tact in such moments to get what you want without having to explain that what you want is something worth putting in the paper, something that will place the man in his frame of reference. For most of us such an examination is likely to be deflationary; a man who has read his own obituary will never be quite the same again.

Not even if he is a man of consequence, who gets a creditable amount of space in the paper. Almost certainly, to run over this sketch of his life as seen by a stranger will be a melancholy exercise; he will know that some of his achievements have been overestimated, he will be disgusted to find that the accomplishments in which he has taken most pride do not seem very important to an outsider; and here and there some phrase, set down in all innocence, will be a bitter reminder of some of the things he had always intended to do, and never got round to. Viewed objectively, compared with the history of the general run of men, it may be a re-

spectable record; but its subject cannot view it objectively, he must compare it not with what other men have
accomplished, but with what he intended to accomplish
when he started out. Few men can make that comparison with any great satisfaction.

Of the length and nature of my obituary, now in type
in certain New York newspaper offices, I know nothing;
all I can be sure of is that it is longer than I deserve, for
it is a tradition of the trade that both newspapermen and
ex-newspapermen always get more space than they are
really worth on the obituary page. But whatever its
length and implications, I have no regrets that I escaped
reading it, by however narrow a margin, after the late
New England hurricane.

III

It is not my purpose to tell you about the hurricane.
No cataclysm of Nature, except possibly Noah's flood,
ever afflicted a region populated by so many professional
writers; and most of them were prompt to cash in on it,
especially if they carried no wind insurance and had
to compensate their losses somehow. Already I have
read five magazine articles about it; an account of it
will be the climactic chapter in two novels that are to be
published before you read this, and God knows how
many more in preparation. I can only hope that the

novelists will remember from personal experience that the hurricane fell alike on the just and on the unjust, and will not use it as a *deus ex machina* which removes all the undesirable characters while the hero and heroine come through unscathed. For there have been novels in which hurricanes, earthquakes, volcanic eruptions, etc., displayed as sure a marksmanship and as careful a discrimination as the United States Marines.

Two gentlemen from upper New Hampshire have testified in *Harper's* that, in that remote region, people were slow to realize the extent and gravity of the catastrophe. So, it must be confessed, were some of us on the Connecticut shore, right in the middle of things. When a hurricane is over you know that you are not dead; you realize it so vividly—especially if there had been some doubt about your survival, for a while—that it may not occur to you that people at a distance do not share your knowledge. It happened that no one was killed in the small community where I was living, that no one I knew personally was among the casualties in the near-by towns that suffered far more serious damage; and while we knew things had been pretty bad in our neighborhood, it took time to grasp the dimensions of the disaster, to perceive that when hundreds had been killed over a wide area, most of the millions who had not been killed were going to be worried about till definitely reported safe.

The process by which one is reported dead is simple

and logical enough. One's friends call up the papers, asking, "What do you hear about X?" The wires being down, they have naturally heard nothing about X. Thus X is unreported, therefore X is missing; and a reading public unfamiliar with hurricanes draws the natural analogy from local and minor disasters, fires and train wrecks and so on, in which those at first reported missing usually turn out to be dead. So it happened that on the Saturday morning after the hurricane, when the yard had been cleaned up and the roads were open and we were ready to go back to town, the New York papers at last got into the devastated area, and I learned that I was missing. But that was only the beginning.

It was due to the generosity of my friends in the trade that I was posted as missing on the front page, in a position and size of type about equivalent to that allotted, on the other side of the page, to the mobilization of the Czechoslovak army (nobody could have dreamed that day that the two pieces of news would turn out to be of equal inconsequence). But it is a thoroughly natural presumption that a man missing in large headlines must be more completely missing than somebody whose unreportedness is buried in the body of the story. So in that day's evening papers the possibility was verging on certainty; and one of the radio stations, I am told, went to the length of reporting that my corpse had been seen floating out to sea.

And that was the end of the story. Between the hurricane and Hitler, the papers and the broadcasting stations were overloaded that week; there was little time or space for the correction of misapprehensions. News is the unusual, the not-to-be-expected; so I suppose I have no right to complain if it was news that Davis was dead, but not news, not worth putting in the papers, that Davis was not dead after all. The implications, however, are by no means flattering; and it all entailed a good deal of inconvenience to my friends. My wife for some reason was not listed as missing—somewhat illogically, for a hurricane, like an air raid, is no respecter of women and children; my friends drew the natural conclusion that she was somewhere else and began to ask her about me by telephone and telegraph. But, believing that I was dead but not quite sure, they were driven to all sorts of circumlocutions; trying to find language that was neither callous enough to grieve her if she were a widow, nor ominous enough to alarm her if she did not yet know whether she was or not.

To the friends I met after I came back to town the inconvenience was of another and perhaps graver sort. On each man's face I could see a look of startled surprise, not altogether unmixed with resentment; for they had done their grieving for Davis, and it could not but be regarded as an imposition when they discovered that it was all a mistake, and that some day they would have it to do over again. My contemporaries are approaching the time of life when to hear of the unexpected death of a friend is as common as it was in war days; and if you have work to do you cannot spend too much time worrying about it. When you hear that good old X is dead you put in perhaps two minutes thinking hard about good old X, and hoping that he left enough for his widow to live on; after which you put him out of your mind and get down to business, so that you may leave enough for your widow to live on when your time comes. Now and then in later life of course you will think of X again—when you see some piece of news in the paper that he would have particularly appreciated or particularly detested; when your partner misses a slam that X would have made if he had been playing the hand; or when recurrently you have to try to find a job for his widow, in case he didn't leave enough for her to live on.

But that is about all, except in the rare instances of some personality so vivid that when it is gone the landscape never looks quite so bright again. (Such, in my experience, were Guy Holt, Don Marquis, and Max Swain; such, I gather, was Elinor Wylie to those who knew her well; so indeed, as a personality rather than an artist, William Shakespeare seems to have been chiefly remembered by his friends.) But most of us do not rate so much remembrance, except by those to whom our passing means a radical change in all the circumstances of life; this is the world of the living, and there would be no time to live if we spent too much time thinking about the dead. Two minutes when the news is heard and an occasional passing recollection thereafter is about as much mourning as the average man can reasonably expect from most of those who knew him; it is entirely intelligible if my friends feel that they have done their mourning for me and owe me no more grief at any later date, when the story can no longer be denied.

IV

It appears also that practically all of my friends have read Mark Twain, or at least heard him quoted; for they were few indeed who, on seeing me reappear in the flesh, did not remark that the report seemed to have been greatly exaggerated. Endeavoring to escape that cliché, I contented myself with saying when comment was called for that it was at least premature; but I begin to wonder if that is altogether true.

For if I remember correctly the science I once studied (and if it has not since then been turned upside down, as other sciences have been), from the biologist's point of view we start dying the moment we are born—which is only another way of saying that every organism exists in time as well as in space, that it is not quite the same at any moment as it was the moment before. So, if I have an actuarial expectation of another quarter century of life, about two-thirds of all that will ever have been Davis has gone past already; from the time angle, I am two-thirds dead.*

I do not pretend to have any clear idea of what Time is (or Space either); Sir Arthur Eddington's famous diagram of the Present as a moving point between the infinite cones of the Past and the Future may mean something to Eddington, but it does not help the layman much. H. G. Wells, lately correcting in the *Saturday Review of Literature* the too extensive inferences that some people drew from the concept of Time as the fourth dimension which he once presented in *The Time Machine,* remarks that Time differs from other dimensions in that you can travel along it in only one direction. (And, it might be added, you must travel in that direction, at ever-increasing speed, whether you like it or not. As Don Marquis said about being fifty, a couple of years later you are sixty, and ten minutes after that you are eighty-five.)

Wells adds that "we live in measurable bits of time," but very small bits apparently, and quotes a suggestion of Sir Edwin Ray Lankester that perhaps "our brain cells

---

* Charlie Merrill tells me that Montaigne thought of this before I did. But I leave it in the text; it is true enough to be passed along, for the benefit of others who have not read Montaigne.

live for an instant as the blood and fresh oxygen pulse to them and then become inactive till the next heartbeat reawakens them." Maybe so; at any rate it is obviously an unwarranted simplification to speak of a personality. If the brain lives in each fresh heartbeat, a man who has lived seventy years is a sequence of something like two and a half billion transitory personalities, whose resemblance is sometimes close and sometimes remote. The conclusion is substantially true even if the premise be a little shaky, as almost anybody can testify when meeting an old friend after ten years' separation. He is not the man he used to be—maybe better, probably worse, but certainly not the same.

The photographer can abstract the outward appearance of a single one of these personalities from the rest, but only the outward appearance; we habitually talk as if we could manage a sort of psychic photography, grasping the personality as it is at the moment; but it will not look quite the same to any two observers, no outsider can penetrate very deep, and in any case what you are trying to photograph is changing under your eyes much more rapidly than its outward appearance. To take an obvious instance—a man may look pretty much the same, changed in expression no doubt but not in feature, the moment after he has been fired from a job he had held twenty years and expected to hold for the rest of his life, as he looked the moment before. But he is not the same and will never be the same again; even if he gets a better job and keeps it, the shock, the reminder of insecurity, the loss of prestige will have left permanent scars on all of his successive personalities thereafter.

Because our psychic mechanism is such that we must live for the most part in the present, we cannot manage this concept of the individual as a moving and changing picture; as a working hypothesis we must abstract the average of a comparatively few of his personalities and say, "That is the man." We used to omit his childhood from the excerpt, but the psychologists have taught us that that is a mistake; we still omit as a rule his old age, or the years after his activity has slowed down, for whatever reason; when we think of Napoleon we think of the average of all the Napoleons, say from 1795 to 1815; but we leave the six years between Waterloo and his death out of account. Yet the fat and ailing gentleman who lived on St. Helena was Napoleon; not the Napoleon of 1796 or of 1807 (again one must simplify, for there were many Napoleons in each of those years), but certainly *a* Napoleon—and indeed a Napoleon who had considerable effect on the subsequent history of Europe. A good many of the second guesses by spinning which he whiled away his leisure on St. Helena were woven into the fabric—the ideal if not the real fabric—of the Second Empire.

A rough average of a period of months or years is likely to be not so very far wrong as a working hypothesis; but our craving for stability is apt to make us forget how soon even these provisional abstractions become outdated. Hitler has displayed an unusual continuity of purpose and fixity of ideas, but the post-Munich Hitler is not, cannot be, the pre-Munich Hitler; such a triumph as he won in September 1938 by the superior force of his personality must have its effect on what is loosely called the character of any man.* It is nonsense to speak of the Lincoln of 1864; even with the crudest of abstractions there were half a dozen successive Lincolns in 1864. To be sure in Lincoln, as in most other individuals, there were certain characteristics that changed much more slowly, so slowly that we may think of them as perma-

---

* As it certainly did. Why should Hitler have seized what was left of Czechoslovakia six months after he had promised the world to leave it alone, when he could have dominated Central Europe by subtler means without disillusioning the appeasers? No rational explanation will hold water; the only plausible theory is that his unbroken triumphs had engendered in him that confident insolence that the Greeks called *hubris*. In Greek tragedy it was invariably punished, and usually in Greek history as well: from which optimists have drawn the conclusion that Hitler too, having gone too far, must meet with retribution. It would be unsafe to suppose that there is any must about it; the laws of art are not necessarily valid in the world of events, and the historical instances are too few for confident induction. Genghis Khan also went too far, and then kept right on going.

nent features of character. But of the manifestations of these traits the most that can truly be said is that some things are a little less impermanent than others.

V

We do not like to think of these matters, as a rule, because it is unpleasant to be reminded that we seem to be subject, like the rest of the cosmos, to the Second Law of Thermodynamics; that we are steadily running down. For a while, in some respects, the trend of the curve may be upward; the Shakespeare (an abstraction from innumerable momentary Shakespeares) who wrote *Hamlet* was not the Shakespeare who wrote *Love's Labour's Lost;* we say he was a better and greater Shakespeare, but it may not have seemed so to the self-observing mechanisms of that personality; he must have known that he was older, that he tired more easily; he had learned a good many things in the intervening years that could have been no fun for him to find out, however they broadened and deepened his understanding. But sooner or later for every man the curve turns downward, unless he escapes the misfortune of living too long by what may be the almost equally serious misfortune of dying too soon. (To this fairly obvious truth more attention might be paid by the income tax laws, which permit deductions for "the exhaustion, wear and tear, including

obsolescence, of property used in the trade or business,"
unless that property happens to be a man's own energies
and own brain.)

Somewhere in each human being's life there must be
an optimum point, a moment when the average of all
his successive personalities is higher than it ever was
before, or will ever be again. But he can never identify
that point himself; whether things to date have been
good or bad, he usually hopes and very often believes
that they are going to be better. Nor can outsiders discern that optimum point except in retrospect, and then
none too confidently. Lincoln, almost alone among great
men, seems to have died exactly at his peak; the average
of all the Lincolns was higher on April 14, 1865, than it
had ever been before—or might ever have been again.

Most people no doubt live too long—yet you cannot
always be sure that even the elderly have lived long
enough. It might have seemed to John Quincy Adams,
leaving the White House in his sixty-second year—the
first of Presidents, except his father, to be denied reelec-
tion—that he had passed his peak, that the average of
all the John Quincy Adamses would never stand so high
again; yet a good deal of the best of John Quincy Adams
was still to come. Julius Caesar's average might be
higher if he had died a year or two earlier, before he had
been too much infected by Cleopatra's ideas—or it might
be higher if he had lived another twenty years.

These examples from the great may seem remote from a discussion of the average man, but they have their bearing. When we say that X is dead we mean the average of all the X's—an average different for each observer, and none of them perhaps very close to the average that might be computed by Omniscience. But what the phrase really implies is that a moving picture has ended, that the succession of innumerable more or less different X's has stopped, there will never be any more of them. Going into the movie theater you ask the usher if the feature is over; no, he says, it is only half over. So when a middle-aged man says in a moment of weariness that he is half dead, he is telling the literal truth.

To say then that the report of my death was premature was to speak inexactly; it would have been more correct to say that it was two-thirds true, or perhaps even more. For at least two-thirds of all the Davises have passed on and are not coming back. (A good many men, and women, have tried sometimes to resurrect one of those vanished personalities, but without success; the best you can hope for is to find, as did the hero of *Conrad in Quest of His Youth,* something roughly similar, and approximately as satisfactory.) The young man who was mistakenly reported to have been drowned in 1916, himself an average impression created on the senses by the rapid succession of thousands of bits of film, is dead, and I cannot regret him very much; he was a good deal of an ass, he muffed some excellent opportunities—yet he had possibilities that his successors might have realized, and did not. Of those successors some few, I hope, were worth being remembered a little, and missed a little; but more than I like to think of are well buried, with no tears shed even by the current average who inherits what is loosely termed their identity.

To go away, said some Frenchman, is to die a little; true enough, but to stay where you are is also to die a little; in the midst of life we are in death, and the fear of dying (for there are people who fear dying in itself, aside from the pain and inconvenience of the final illness) ought to be mitigated by the reflection that we are dying all the time, and that most of the job has already been done. Few of the people I know are afraid of death, except as it might affect persons or institutions more or less dependent on them; which means that what they are afraid of is not death but the cessation of activity and usefulness. With regard to that not much can be said except that it is going to happen to us all some day, no matter how much we dislike the idea; and that to worry about it in advance is likely to make it happen all the sooner.

At any rate, the next time I am reported dead I shall not dignify the rumor with a denial. If it is not yet entirely true, people will find that out in due time.

Notes on a New Bible

NOTES ON A NEW BIBLE

THE mere suggestion that a new Bible is needed may offend the devout. What, they will ask, is the matter with the old Bible? Well, the chief thing the matter with it is that nobody reads it. The clergy read it, of course, though they are increasingly given to preaching about something else; a good many children are still exposed to carefully chosen bits of it in Sunday school; and some people read it for its literary or historical or psychological value, as they might read Lucretius or Thucydides. There are others who may or may not read it now, but know it because in childhood they were nourished daily on the sincere milk of the Word. But those people are over forty—most of them over sixty; and not many of them have imposed a similar discipline on their children.

If you doubt this try it on your friends, especially your younger friends. See how many intelligent, educated moderns can identify even the commonest Scriptural quotations or allusions. They may recognize the language as "Biblical English," but they will rarely be able to tell

you who said it, or in what context. A few decades ago
the Bible was the cornerstone of an education; whatever else a cultured man knew, he knew that first; and
the unlettered were likely to know it even if they knew
no other book. But the faith that rested on the infallible
Word has faded, and knowledge of the Word inevitably
faded with it.

The Fundamentalists may still profess to believe the
Bible from cover to cover, but in a world so full of other
things they find less time than their ancestors found for
reading it. The intellectual wing of modern Protestantism seems to regard the Bible somewhat as students of
politics regard the writings of the Founding Fathers of
this republic—the views of able and earnest men on
topics of major importance, valuable not only in themselves but for their sentimental associations; but to be
used with caution as a guide to the problems of our
times. That is a sensible way to regard the writings of the
fathers, sacred or profane; but it is no way to get the
general public to read them. Most readers of this, whatever their attitude toward religion in general, will probably feel that the loss of faith in the inerrancy of Holy
Writ is in itself a symptom of improvement in the human
mind. But, as usual, we obtained this freedom at a
price. Quite aside from its religious content, the Bible
had values that are almost lost, and there seems little
hope of their recovery.

I am speaking, as any American Protestant must, of the Bible in English, the King James Version, and of the unique position which it held for three centuries in British and American culture. The Fundamentalist theological student who refused to learn Greek on the ground that "if English was good enough for Jesus Christ it is good enough for me" may be a figment of invention, but the story dramatizes a truth more important than any question as to the language Jesus used. The cultural background, the intellectual and emotional subsoil of English-speaking Protestants is not what the writers of Scripture (good, bad, and indifferent as writers go) actually said, but the magnificent if sometimes inaccurate English into which the translators of the Authorized Version rendered it—chapter headings and all.

To anyone brought up in that tradition the Bible in Latin (though it too is part of our cultural background) seems somewhat less authoritative, and the Bible in French or German is hardly the Bible at all. The Greek and Hebrew originals, I suppose, grow familiar to scholarly clergymen who use them daily; but a reader who has no Hebrew and has made only casual excursions into New Testament Greek feels that the actual words of Luke and Paul sound less like the Bible even than the Latin Vulgate, to say nothing of the King James Version. Such a phrase as "the abomination of desolation" means something to anyone familiar with the English Bible, though probably not what it meant to the Jews who invented it; whereas *to bdelygma tes eremoseos* is only an echo from a college examination paper.

That is our Bible—not what the prophets and evangelists actually said, but what King James's translators made of it, with the interpretations, sometimes right and sometimes wrong, that generations of the devout have read into it. Occasionally it misrepresents the originals, not so often with its faults as with its splendors. Professor Goodspeed of Chicago, in the introduction to his translation of the New Testament into modern idiom, remarks that it was not written in literary Greek (though St. Luke wrote well, and St. Paul too) but in "the common language of everyday life," and that consequently it should be translated into the same sort of language. The men who wrote it had something to say which they considered of primary importance, and they were unconcerned about their style except to make sure that people understood them. Goodspeed's translation has an undeniable power—the power of the original, the power that comes from single-minded earnestness and clarity. But it does not sound like the Bible.

To have something to say and to say it as clearly as you can is the best recipe for a good style; and the writers of the New Testament had it. But the translators of the Authorized Version had something else, something more

like magic. The magic may have lain in the incompar-
able richness of Elizabethan English, or it may lie in
the three centuries of tradition that intervene between
our time and theirs. But whatever it comes from, it is
there. Goodspeed's straightforward rendering must
hold you by its content, if it holds you at all; and for
most of us that hold is gone.

The book that for three centuries was known to every
English-speaking person who knew any book at all derived its authority from its content, of course, in the day
when everybody was a Fundamentalist. Its ethical effect
on a people who took the teachings of Jesus and the
braggart bluster of the primitive Yahweh as equally inspired, and equally authoritative, was perhaps more bad
than good; its value as cultural history was long obscured
by dogma; but its value as literature was immense and
irreplaceable. It was the only great literature with which
the average man ever came into contact. If other great
literature happened to come his way he might ignore it,
as hard to comprehend and alien to his interest; but he
struggled to comprehend the Bible, at its hardest and
most alien. He did that not because it was literature,
but because it was the Word of God; but he could not
help getting some purely cultural values out of it. That
so many able men sprang from nowhere in the early days
of this republic may have been due to the sudden release
of biological and economic repressions; but that so many

of them who had little or no education could talk well
and write well was due chiefly to the fact that they had
read one book and reread it till they were drenched in its
language.

And when they quoted or adapted its language people
knew what they were talking about. The Bible provided
a common cultural background that had as much value
as an extra language, and a language of great richness;
every Scriptural allusion called up a whole chain of associated ideas. For the educated, another such background
was provided by the Greek and Latin classics. Till fifty
years ago in this country, till twenty-five or thirty years
ago in Great Britain, a quotation from St Paul or Isaiah,
from Vergil or Horace, was at once a short cut and an
evocation of endless resonances; it enriched the melody
with orchestration.

If there is flatness and aridity in modern writing it
may be due to the vanishing of those two great common
denominators of culture. A contemporary writer in
English has the feeling of working in two dimensions
where his predecessors worked in three or four—especially in this country, where the only literary allusions
that can be made with any confidence that they will be
generally recognized are to the works of Amos and
Andy.* The English seem to be almost as badly off;

---

* Perhaps, after seven years, Edgar Bergen might be added.

their schools still teach the classics, though not so much as they used to, but their speakers and writers no longer quote them. Rudyard Kipling may go down in histories of English literature as the last important writer who really knew his Bible. The trade of writing would be easier and more agreeable, the pastime of reading would be more remunerative, if those common backgrounds existed still; but science which has made our lives so much more comfortable, and has at least begun to brush the cobwebs from our minds, has exacted its price. There is so much more to learn nowadays that hardly anybody has time to study Horace or Thucydides unless he expects to make his living by teaching them; and the Bible is read for pleasure only by the rare eccentrics who would read Horace or Thucydides for pleasure.

II

There will always be people like that, but it seems impossible that the Bible can ever again be the book of a whole people. Our ancestors did not read it for pleasure; they read it to learn the way of life. People stopped reading it when they began to suspect that the way of life could be better learned elsewhere, or to doubt if there is any way of life at all. Nothing could be written now that could make any plausible pretense to supernatural authority; a substitute Bible would have to gain readers solely on its own merits.

Obviously, then, there can be no substitute for the King James Bible as a cultural influence; nobody can write such English any more, and if it could be written only lovers of good writing would read it. But the Bible has its religious aspects too; and from that point of view it can perhaps be, if not replaced, at any rate supplemented by something more useful to our time than the Mosaic cosmogony or the prophetic interpretation of history. A new Bible could never mean to anybody what the old Bible has traditionally meant to the orthodox— the inerrant, sufficient, and final message of God to man, not to be added unto or taken away from under penalty of plagues and reprobation. But it could mean what the original nucleus of the Bible meant to the Hebrews before the Exile—a guide, as accurate as could then be constructed, to the way of life as then conceived. There was no abhorrence of profane knowledge in those days; the writers of the earliest Bible did not have much of it but they used what they had. As surely as any modern rationalist, they were convinced that the way of life depended on a correct understanding of man's relation to the universe. They wrote an account of that relation, including interpretation of the past and forecast of the future, based on the knowledge which they had and subject to such revision as the increase of their knowledge required. There is no reason why twentieth-century writers cannot do the same; some, whom I shall presently discuss, have already done it.

A new Bible for our time must be at least negatively limited by science; it might speculate with more or less confidence in extra-scientific fields but it could not affirm what science denied. Considering that science has got into the habit of denying what it affirmed yesterday, and will deny tomorrow what it affirms today, it may seem a waste of labor to try to write a scientific Bible at all. Any speculation as to the future of man must take into consideration a range of millions, if not billions, of years; it begins to seem as if all the time there is will not be too much for evolution to distil the traces of the primitive anthropoid out of us. And just at present the most respected scientists think that there is not going to be nearly as much time as they hoped for a few years ago. "Looked at in terms of time," wrote Jeans in the spring of 1929, "the message of astronomy is one of endless possibility and hope." But by the fall of 1931 Jeans had come to the conclusion that the end of all things is several trillion years nearer than he had previously supposed.

But Jeans and Eddington, who then agreed with him, may just as well have been wrong that time as the time before. At any rate, we can do nothing but work as well as we can with the most plausible knowledge we have.

That was what the writers of the first Bible did; the man
who wrote the (probably earlier) story of the Creation
in the second chapter of Genesis thought that this was
most probably the way it happened, and the man who
wrote the divergent story which we read in the first
chapter thought he knew better. (The final editor who
left them both in the definitive text, as a stumbling-block
to later literalists, may have been a scrupulous person
who could not make up his mind which was more
plausible and decided to let his readers take their
choice.) You may think that if Jeans and Eddington
refuse to allow us time enough for evolution, and if
Planck and Schrödinger and Heisinger have upset the
laws of human thought, we might as well go down to
the corner barroom and get drunk instead of worrying
about the way of life. But you will not find Jeans and
Eddington in the corner pub, or Planck and Schrödinger
and Heisinger in the neighborhood *Bierstube;* they have
returned to their laboratories to go on from there and
see what else they can find out It may be a little less
lugubrious next time.

Any Bible starting from their findings would need
frequent revision; but so did the first Bible. There was
no unalterable canon in those days; whosoever got the
upper hand in politics could rewrite the Scriptures to
fit his own ideas. Truth was not the facts as men of old
had set them down, but their interpretation from the

enlightened modern point of view of King Josiah's time. The writers of a new Bible must be considerably more scrupulous about the record, but substantially they would be doing the same thing for the same purpose—setting down an account of man's relation to the universe, an interpretation of the past and a forecast of the future, as a guide to the way of life.

III

The sole contribution of ancient Israel to universal culture, says Bertholet, was the teleological interpretation of history—the explanation of what has happened by what is going to happen, the construing of the historic process in relation to its goal. As usually practiced this has been the worst of human errors, because men put the cart before the horse; they discerned the goal by revelation or intuition and then doctored the record to fit. Pious historians who thought that the Hebrew people was the destined heir of all the ages—or the Roman people, or the German people, or the American people, or the Nordic race, or the adherents of some variety of Christian doctrine—have explained the past as only a prologue to this foreordained consummation; and foreigners have been duly slaughtered or heretics burned to make the problem work out to the answer given in the back of the book.

This happened because teleology was concerned with what God meant to do with man (each teleologist, of course, being certain that God's purpose was identical with his own). Teleology might be a useful tool if we turned it around and tried to find out from a candid study of the past what man may be able to make of himself. Evolution seems to be tending to some goal which we do not yet discern; and man may possibly be able to influence it, and its goal with it, if he can bring himself to spend as much time on self-improvement as he does on the improvement of dahlias and race horses. The interpretation of the process and the concept of the goal are still as humanly fallible as those of the authors of Deuteronomy and Revelations; but we know that they are human and are ready to revise them when they prove false, as were the ancient Hebrews until the disastrous end of King Josiah perverted the teleological interpretation of history into an apologia for the past mistakes of the interpreters.

Does this leave God out? Only the God of the traditionalists. There is room in the scheme, if you like, for the God of the Modernists, whether you consider him the senior partner in humanity's collective venture or only a distillate of man's best aspirations. And that other God—the vaster, bleaker, inscrutable God of Neo-Spinozism, the God Who is the universe—the scheme has room for him too; the only question is whether it has room for anything else. A Spinozist interpretation of history must take into account God's purpose for man to this extent—that we do not know and probably shall never know what that purpose is, or if God considers man at all; that at any moment God-the-Universe may see fit to abolish us for no reason that we can comprehend; that in all his endeavors man can count on no more than the insecure freedom of a prisoner out on bail. This will not be a popular creed till the human race is a good deal farther along; but I believe it is what we must come to, and a few men have already had the courage to grapple with its toughest implications.

One of these is General J. C. Smuts, whose presidential address delivered to the British Association for the Advancement of Science attacked the problem of reconciling the history of man who is trying to climb up with the history of a universe that seems to be running down. He did not solve it—perhaps nobody will ever solve it—but at least he looked it in the eye. "While the smaller world of life seems on the whole to be on the upgrade the larger physical universe is on the downgrade. . . . In life and mind Nature seems to have discovered a secret which enables her to irradiate with imperishable glory the decay to which she is physically doomed." He observes that "beauty and holiness are as much aspects of Nature as energy and entropy," but he does not shut his eyes to the fact that the majority tendency in the universe, so far as we can now see it, is downward.

Perhaps this address, and anything else that could now be written, could be no more than source material for the first draft of a new Bible. The two men who first practiced the teleological interpretation of history are so far forgotten that scholars know them only as J and E, but out of fragments of their work the Old Testament is largely built. Now recent years have seen two interpretations of history in the light of modern teleology. H. G. Wells's *Outline of History* purports to be a record of fact; Johannes V. Jensen's *The Long Journey* is a work of the creative imagination; but there is a good deal of history and a good deal of imaginative creation in both, and they are both interpretations of man's past in terms of purely human purpose.

They are good beginnings, but hardly more. Mankind in Wells's book is only a magnified Wells. Jensen's story is a magnificent dramatization of tons of anthropological data, but it is as rigorously and exclusively a Nordic Bible as the Old Testament (barring a few passages in the Prophets) is a Hebrew Bible. You do not need to be, or think you are, a Nordic to get a high emotional value out of the story of the man who, when all the rest of the tribe was fleeing southward from the spreading cold, turned stubbornly back, and learned to live on the ice. But Jensen's climax is the voyage of Columbus; and when he makes Columbus a Lombard, with a Visigothic crew, you can see that he is as determined as Ezra and Nehemiah to exclude the uncircumcised from the congregation of the Lord.

One experience with the consequences of trying to universalize a primitive and purely nationalist Bible ought to be enough. Wells and Jensen have broken the ice; but the J and E of our new Bible are not yet born.

IV

But the teleology includes not only the past but the future, not only history but apocalypse. The naïve faith of a true apocalypse can hardly be recovered now; but men may still speculate on the future, and if their speculations are informed with that "emotional attitude toward the universe as a whole" that J. B. S. Haldane sets down as one of the essential elements of religion, they may be not mere inventions but myths. "A true myth," says W. Olaf Stapledon, "is one which within the universe of a certain culture expresses richly, and often perhaps tragically, the highest admirations possible within that culture." Here again Wells broke the ice. His interest lies now in the near future; but Haldane and Stapledon who have tried their hand at creation of myths of the remote future might never have done it but for his example.

Haldane's myth, *The Last Judgment,* appeared a few years ago; it was limited in space and in objective, but within those limitations it was a very creditable specimen of apocalyptic vision. Stapledon's *Last and First Men* is a much longer book; and if he could write like the Wells of thirty years ago it could be put into a modern Bible as it stands. Stapledon admits that present knowledge is rudimentary and that his forecast of the future may seem, even to the next generation, laughably naïve. But there are spiritual values in the Old Testament prophets, rudimentary and naïve as their knowledge seems to us. Stapledon's guesses may be mostly wrong but he gets his teeth into the central problem of philosophy and morals—the apparent antipathy between human striving and the direction of the universe, between man's will and God's. We have not made much progress with that problem since the Old Testament was written, and we may not be much farther along when Stapledon is as ancient as Job.

Haldane had no room for discussion of the immediate future; he assumed world federation, world peace, world prosperity, and the unbroken progress of man's conquest of Nature until evolution ceased because the human race had everything it wanted. After millions of years that Golden Age came to an end; the use of tidal power had drawn the moon toward the earth, to disintegrate at last in a rain of rocks and fire which made the planet uninhabitable. Most of the human race ("un-able," as Haldane remarks, "to look a million years ahead") sat and waited for the catastrophe in resigna-tion, or in optimistic hope that it would never really happen; but a forward-looking minority explored Venus and directed the evolution of its descendants to fit them for life on that not very hospitable planet. There a select and disciplined few were able to found a new human race, far more serious-minded, to which the individual was nothing, the collective determination everything—a race which could look forward to such accomplishment as the selfish individualists of earth could never have en-visaged.

"Man's little world," says Haldane, "will end. If humanity can enlarge the scope of its will as it has en-larged the reach of its intellect, it will escape that end." So it will, if God-the-Universe remains neutral. Haldane assumes that He will; in a brief study the assumption was perhaps necessary, but Haldane seems an optimist by temperament. Lately he has professed faith in a God much like the deity of the Modernists—an efflorescence of man's highest resolves called forth by the presence of a crisis; apparently a God who, like the Fire Department, works only when somebody turns in an alarm. No one can say this is not so; and certainly in *The Last Judgment* Haldane carries his readers a long way and shows them a spacious and noble vision.

But Stapledon goes vastly farther in space and time and opens up a prospect of frigid and inhospitable magnificence. The ancient Hebrews thought that no man could look on the Face of God and live. Only a brave man could look on the face of a Spinozist God and want to live; but Stapledon has tried it. If more men keep on trying it, even though like Moses they are permitted to see only God's back parts, we may begin to get a little farther along.

V

Haldane's myth carried man forward forty million years, and assumed that our species would attain to such perfection as its nature permits and stay there, till the transit to Venus necessitated the evolving of a new breed of men. Stapledon covers two billion years, in the course of which evolution, sometimes spontaneous and sometimes directed, created eighteen successive human species before an incalculable and inexplicable eruption of nearby stars—an apparently arbitrary gesture of God-the-Universe—extinguished man forever. Meanwhile there had been a removal to Venus when the moon's disintegration was impending, and a further removal to Neptune when the approaching collision of the sun with a mass of dark gas promised to make the inner planets uninhabitable. Neptune was the *ne plus ultra,* even for the men of two billion years hence; when the whole solar system began to go to pieces there was no other place to go.

This vision of the future is simply the past enormously magnified—a recurrent rhythm of catastrophe and recovery, a series of brilliant cultures that rise and flourish and wane and fall, with long dark ages between. It seems more plausible than a continuous upward progress; especially in these present times, when people are wondering if man's intellect is capacious enough to control his inventions, and if his emotions are anywhere near stable enough to control his brain. *Last and First Men* sets the attainment of emotional maturity far in the future, after dark ages that covered nearly ten million years. What became of the First Men, the species to which we have the dubious honor to belong? Well, they did not immediately wipe themselves out in air wars, as so many gloomy prophets of today are predicting; they created a world state under American domination that lasted four thousand years. But before that a series of air wars had pretty thoroughly wiped out Europe and the skepticism and "dispassionate yet creative intelligence" which Stapledon finds more common in Europe than in America.

The America that bested all its rivals was given over to a dogmatic religion blended of Behaviorism, Fundamentalism, and the worship of motion; the American-

ized world state was a sort of Greater Los Angeles whose
dominant interests were sport, piety, and legalized forni-
cation. Thought was a crime, and capacity for thought
was virtually extinct (a few Jews retained it, but were
shrewd enough not to excite prejudice by exercising it) ;
so when the oil and coal were exhausted men lacked the
brains to find a new source of power, and their civilization collapsed. Of later human races one learned how
to disintegrate the atom before it learned how to be careful, and in consequence disintegrated most of the earth's
surface and population. The Second Men, most attractive of all to the present-day reader (since they were all
that the best men of our time vainly aspire to be), were
overthrown by recurrent invasions of the Martians; the
Fifth Men flourished brilliantly till they had to move to
Venus, where the strain of adaptation degraded their
descendants for ages to a sub-human level; the Ninth
Men similarly degenerated after the removal to Neptune; and so on.

Catastrophe and degeneration are possible; the history
of Rome and Knossos, the legends of Atlantis are proof
enough of that. If there has never yet been a world catastrophe, it is perhaps only because there has never yet
been a world culture. But recovery is part of the record
too; after most catastrophes man has recovered, however
slowly and painfully, and recommenced the long climb
upward. Some day that evolutionary trend may eradi-

cate the faults that make us the architects of our own catastrophes; loyalty to the trend and determination to help it along if you can must be the essence of future ethics—as it has been, if not always explicitly, of the best ethics of the past.

But that is only half the story. Even if we learn how to end war, abolish poverty, stamp out disease, and build the New Jerusalem on earth, we are still prisoners out on bail; helpless in the hand of the God-Universe if He chooses to close that hand on us. This is the theme of Stapledon's myth, which only dramatized what he had already set forth more compactly and technically in *A Modern Theory of Ethics.* "Much that seemed very bad to Queen Victoria," he writes, "is judged by us to be very good. Yet the difference between Queen Victoria's horizon and our own is perhaps less than the difference between us and the span of all being."* This is pure Spinozism; what seems bad to us may seem good to the God-Universe, and vice versa. The philosopher is content to acknowledge the contradiction; but the moralist has to try to make people like it, and that is not so easy. Spinoza thought that if you only understand the universe well enough you must love it; and his disciple

---

* For that matter some things that looked good, or at least harmless, when Stapledon wrote, begin to look pretty sour now. But Stapledon would never have claimed that he, any more than Victoria, was infallible.

Lippmann accepts that solution with a rather appalling nonchalance. Agony and disaster are very interesting; the man of insight will appreciate their intellectual beauty and won't care how much they hurt. Stapledon fights it out on the same line and goes a good deal farther. I cannot say he is convincing, but at least he realizes that agony and disaster are not to be dismissed with a neatly turned phrase.

Even his First Men were occasionally tortured by the perception of the conflict between "the intransigent loyalty to Life embattled against Death" and their vision of the "alien and supernal beauty" of the Whole. A hundred thousand years after, a new Messiah "saw the game that I was losing, and it was good—good no less to lose than to win. . . . For me as a character in the play the situation was hideous; for me the spectator it had become excellent, within a wider excellence." But he was a rare spirit, born before his time. Millions of years later the finely organized Second Men had their emotional balance upset by the endlessly repeated disasters of the Martian invasion. "Remote generations had earnestly longed to feel the racial tragedy as a factor in the cosmic beauty"; but their descendants did not feel it, doubted if anybody had ever felt it, and even questioned if there were "any such cosmic beauty to be experienced." The Fifth Men, even before the approaching lunar catastrophe overshadowed the future, were tormented in their felicity by reflections on the multitudinous miseries of the past. They believed that "behind the physical order and behind the desires of minds was a fundamental principle whose essence was aesthetic," so they tried to accept whatever happened as part of the universal beauty. But like us feeble primitives, they found it easier to say they accepted than to accept.

The Eighteenth, last and noblest of human races, found themselves in the same dilemma when they unexpectedly faced extinction. They had learned to temper their desires by "relentless admiration of Fate," to enjoy the game whether they won or lost, even to regard the impending annihilation of mankind as "superb though tragic." But man seemed to be the highest product of the cosmic process; if his struggles and agonies were to end in what Fosdick calls "a hopeless cinder heap" the universe was falling short of perfection. So the Eighteenth Men could not reconcile themselves to the prospect that "the cosmos enterprise itself may fail, the full potentiality of the Real may never find expression." Simply, they were disappointed in God, and felt a moral disapproval of Him for not making the most of His opportunities.

But this was an individual emotion. The Eighteenth Men were able to wake occasionally to a racial consciousness; and in that state they felt no distress over their own approaching end, but only "the ecstasy which admires the Real as it is, and accepts its dark-bright form with joy." This ecstasy of acceptance is the core of Stapledon's ethical theory—an emotional experience in which you recognize that the judgments of the Lord, however inexplicable and ruinous, are true, and righteous altogether. No one can argue with an emotional experience; but to justify it intellectually is another matter. I do not know either Lippmann or Stapledon, but from their writings I surmise that Lippmann came to the doctrine of acceptance as the conclusion, however paradoxical, of a course of reasoning; whereas Stapledon had the emotional experience first and then evolved a theory to explain it.*

There is a "cold fervor of acquiescence," he writes in the *Ethics,* in which "we seem to approve of the universe for being." But to approve of the universe either intellectually or morally you must give it the benefit of a considerable doubt, and suppose that it has higher beauties beyond our vision which outweigh the rather deplorable aspect presented to human perception. Most of us would agree with Santayana that what we can see of the universe is interesting but by no means respectable. But go into a fit of ecstasy and you can regard it (as the

---

* I have since learned that this is not true, at least so far as Stapledon's close friends know. Deprived of that explanation, I utterly fail to follow his reasoning.

Eighteenth Men finally did) as a sort of musical compo-
sition which can be appreciated aesthetically. "It is possible," writes Stapledon, "even in the compulsive reaction to pain in one's own flesh, even while helplessly
watching a beloved's pain, to be, precisely in the act of
frenetic revulsion, coldly, brilliantly enlightened not as
to the excellence of pain, but as to the excellence of the
universe." It may be possible; but it is the martyrs, not
the spinners of theory, who must teach us the trick.

This ethical Higher Synthesis gets you into logical difficulties that backfire on your ethics. Biology seems to
move forward but it needs all the help we can give it; if
loyalty to the life struggle is the highest duty, how can
you reconcile it to abject acquiescence in a disaster that
sets the clock back a million years? You may have to
accept disaster because you cannot prevent it; but if you
bind yourself in advance to like it, you can hardly get up
much enthusiasm for an onerous struggle whose hard-
won triumphs you are content to see annulled in the
long run.

Stapledon tries to get around this by holding that there
is no such thing as the long run; ecstasy is (or at least
may be) "a supratemporal hyperbiological fulfilment."
Modern physics is much concerned with "two-way
time"—physical time, which is not what we commonly
call time at all. Ordinary biological time is a one-way
street; the mill can never grind with the water that is

past. But physical time is indifferent to direction. Events have sequence, but you can read the sequence forward or backward. What was still is, and what is to be is already; the present is "caused" by the future as much as by the past.

The revered Einstein (if quoted correctly) has lately declared that it seems mathematically plausible that what we call cause is really an effect, even in the field of human behavior. You do not do a thing because you willed it; you willed it because it was already determined that you were going to do it. Which is to say that aside from the First Cause there is no cause at all; everything that ever happened or ever will happen is an event eternally existent, and ordinary time is a mere illusion. It is only by a trick of false perspective that victory seems to be annulled by subsequent defeat; victory and defeat are alike eternal, so you ought to be satisfied.

Physically this may be sound doctrine, but there is nothing new about it except its name. For two thousand years men have tried without much success to reconcile it with loyalty to the life struggle (otherwise known as the freedom of the will) ; and I do not see that you make the reconciliation any easier by calling it two-way time instead of predestination. If it seems to be true we must hold fast to it, whether it encourages commendable emotions or not; but its relevance to the temporal and biological world we live in is open to doubt. All events may be predestined, but people who assume in practice some freedom of the will are likely to live longer and more comfortably than those who trust that the Lord will provide. A thousand years ago Islam was far ahead of Christendom; that it fell behind is ascribed by historians largely to Moslem acceptance of the doctrine of predestination in an extreme form. The twenty-two runs scored by the Philadelphia Athletics in the World's Series of 1931 may be eternal events, pre- and post-existent, outweighing in supratemporal reality the nineteen runs scored by the St. Louis Cardinals. But on the baser temporal plane the Cardinals so combined their runs as to win four games and the series, and the Athletics had to take the short end of the money.

Many men have reconciled these contradictories to their own satisfaction; but they have done it not by thinking but by an act of faith or a mystic ecstasy. Stapledon says that the Eighteenth Men often reached by pure reason conclusions like those of our mystics, but he does not try to explain how that could happen. It is a statement of his faith, whose fruition is prudently postponed for two billion years and ascribed to the operation of a wholly unprecedented mode of consciousness. Meanwhile those of us who have not risen (or sunk) to the mystic level may find more nourishment in the remark of Henri Fauconnier: "It is preferable that we should not know if our destiny is really the work of our hands. Irresponsible, we should lack fire; responsible, we should agonize with remorse. No religion dares to rescue us from this uncertainty." And the philosophers who dare seem able to rescue no one but themselves.

VI

These criticisms of a theory, however, do not detract from the value of a profound and courageous book. Stapledon has tackled the toughest problem yet encountered by man, and if he has not solved it, neither has anybody else. Books like his we need and shall continue to need as far ahead as any man can see. More and more people are losing faith in the old way of life, and many have come to believe there is no way of life at all. Perhaps not for the individual; but the race is made up of individuals, and if there is hope for the race it means brighter prospects for the individuals of the future in whom our blood will run, and our good intentions may come somewhat nearer fruition.

But it looks as if the way of life is not so much to be found as to be built, through a wilderness at present unmapped; and while not many of us know enough to help with the surveying, we can all lend a hand at the road work. "Most good actions," says Haldane, "merely serve to stave off the inroads of chaos on the human race. The man who creates a new idea, whether expressed in language, art, or invention, may at least be co-operating actively in the plan. The average man cannot do this, but he must learn that the highest of his duties is to assist those who are creating, and the worst of his sins to hinder them." Unfortunately it is not always easy to say what is assistance and what is hindrance. The gentlemen who assured us that the depression was not going to amount to anything meant to assist, but it looks as if they hindered. The Japanese generals now operating in China are apparently hindering, yet no doubt their intentions are of the best. Socrates may have been only half right when he said that virtue is knowledge; but the doctrine has some point in an age when good intentions are fairly common, and knowledge is appallingly rare.

The old Bible showed us, by the lights of its authors, what was help and what was hindrance in the endeavor to get the human race forward. We have somewhat brighter lights at our disposal now and we had better use them. A new Bible must of course for a long time be the book of a few. The masses did not read the old Bible because it was the opinion of wise and earnest men; they read it because it was the Word of God. You cannot make them feel the same way about the word of H. G. Wells or Olaf Stapledon; especially as it promises no eternal bliss for the individual, but only an uncertain hope for the race. But the original Bible must have been the book of a few, and those few brought a whole nation around to their way of thinking; the New Testament was the book of a few, yet it conquered half the world. Some day even the average man may be interested in dispassionate studies of his relation to the Universe; he had better be, unless the inroads of chaos are to overwhelm him before he gets anywhere at all.

The concept of the goal will change as we go on, and so will ideas of the best way to get there; sacred writings of the present and the future will be superseded as the sacred writings of the past are being superseded now. But their values need not be lost. You can get something out of the opening chapters of Genesis even if you do not accept them as literal truth; and the spirit that is in Wells and Jensen, in Stapledon and Haldane will be worth something when their personalities are as completely forgotten as those of J and E.

Let Us Now Praise Famous Men

LET US NOW PRAISE FAMOUS MEN

THERE were brave men before Agamemnon, but they lie unwept and unknown because they and their descendants had no poet on the pay roll; and there were brave men in Agamemnon's day who got a bad break in the publicity. It must have taken a good deal of courage for Thersites, that early champion of the underprivileged, to stand up to the Shepherds of the People and publish inconvenient truths; but as Homer tells it, or whoever rewrote Homer in the days when the Ionian proletariat was beginning to demand the vote, all the glory goes to Odysseus the well-armed strikebreaker. Thersites was very likely an ill bred and disagreeable person, but he could hardly have had all the faults that Homer ascribes to him, in a story as crudely class-angled as a modern "proletarian" novel.

Long after Agamemnon, the reputations of good men were distorted, and some of the distortions have persisted to our time. Our knowledge of ancient history is spotty; for all the labor that has been expended on coins and inscriptions and papyri, books are still the

principal source—such books, good or bad, as have
happened to survive. And no man ever suffered more
gravely from the accidents of survival than Publius
Licinius Egnatius Gallienus—the last gentleman who
was Emperor of Rome (with one brief and negligible
exception); a man to whose tremendous and undissuadable efforts to retrieve what seemed to everybody
else a hopeless civilization we largely owe the presenta-
tion of civilization through the crisis of the third century A. D. What survived, to be sure, was chiefly the
framework and structure; most of the non-essentials
had had to be thrown overboard to keep the ship of
state afloat at all. Culture and prosperity, both pretty
widely diffused at the beginning of the century, had by
its end been restricted to small groups at the top; hope
had gone, about as much as anybody dared expect now
was to keep things as quiet as possible; such speculative
thought as remained had turned into theological chan-
nels, and if religion through the century had become
more philosophical, philosophy had become even more
definitely religious. The "pagan spirit" that some moderns ignorantly worship was about as rare among pagans as among Christians, by the time Rome went over
to Christianity.

 Nevertheless the framework of the Roman order and
the Mediterranean civilization survived, some letters and
education survived; Rome had still two centuries to pass

that on to the German tribes over the border before the border was finally washed out and the barbarians overflowed western Europe. That survival was the achievement of many men, most of them obscure and unknown—soldiers who died fighting back the Goths; civilians trained by centuries of peace in the belief that fighting was no more the layman's business than the practice of medicine, who suddenly discovered when the barbarians were at the door that they *could* fight, for their homes and their families. It was the work of great men too, who got the credit; of the organizing ability of Diocletian and Constantine, who worked with what they had to work with, whether it was what they wanted or not; of the military genius and roughneck energy of Aurelian and Probus, who finally flung the barbarians out and pulled the disintegrating empire back into one piece.

But for what the great men did and for a good deal of what the small men did, in so far as it was effective, Gallienus laid the foundation. He kept his head when all about him were losing theirs and blaming it on him; he held together what he could and wasted no time lamenting what was gone beyond recovery; he began that thorough reorganization of the army and the civil administration which made Aurelian and Constantine possible. That these lines are written in the Latin rather than the Runic alphabet, that indeed we descendants of the tribes who eventually overran western Europe are able to write at all, is due largely to the enormous, unwearying, and till lately unrecognized labors of Gallienus.

II

When he was born, in 218, Rome had already been slipping down for half a century from the all-time high of Antoninus Pius's day. The Mediterranean world had never fully recovered from the great pandemic plague under Marcus Aurelius; on the Rhine and the Danube the Germans were a constantly growing menace; the new Persian Empire in the East, young, aggressive, and inspired by a fanatical religion, was far more formidable than its Parthian predecessor had ever been. And weaknesses in the structure of the Roman government and Mediterranean society, long present but hardly noticed in the days of prosperity, were beginning to be uncomfortably apparent; all Rome's chickens were coming home to roost at once.

Theoretically the Emperor was a magistrate, chosen by the people with the approval of the Senate; in fact, from the very first, the army had acted as representative of the people, and the Senate could only give a perfunctory ratification to the army's choice. This might not have mattered much if the army had been a unit; but it was split into three principal groups—on the Rhine, on the Danube, in Syria—with scattered corps elsewhere; and the death of any Emperor was likely to be the signal for a struggle for power between rival generals, supported—or sometimes pushed on—by rival armies. Septimius Severus, victor in one such struggle a quarter of a century before Gallienus was born, was realist enough to recognize the source of power; and his deathbed advice to his sons, "Keep the soldiers prosperous and don't worry about anything else," was a precept borne in mind by succeeding Emperors—and by their soldiers too, who worried less and less about anything but their own enrichment. Naturally the army found it more profitable to revolt and set up a new Emperor who, if they could make him stick, would hand out a liberal donative to the troops, than to waste too much effort on the defense of the frontiers. Further, in the peaceful days of the previous centuries, the Emperors (for reasons that seemed sound at the time) had abandoned the principle of defense in depth and massed their troops along the borders. Men enlisted, served, retired and died in the same province, and their sons grew up to take their places; which gradually turned the Roman army into a collection of local National Guards with local interests. In case of a great war detachments had to be drawn from, say, the Rhine and the Danube legions to help the Syrian army defend the Euphrates; which was all very well unless there happened to be simultaneous wars on the Rhine and the Danube. In that case the troops wanted, understandably, to stay where they were and defend their homes.

And now the soldiers were drawn almost entirely from the less civilized races and classes of the empire; while their commanders, who were usually also the provincial governors, were selected from the Senatorial aristocracy—itself the distillate and representative of the Graeco-Roman upper classes, the prosperous country-club set and Chamber of Commerce crowd (I borrow Henry Haskell's valid parallel) in every city of the empire. In race, background, and interest there was between commanders and men a growing gulf; the officers the men trusted were those of their own races and their own kind—centurions, or ex-centurions promoted to higher commands.

That was not the sort of army that had conquered the Mediterranean world for Rome. Economically too the government, and the empire, were in a bad way; purchasing power was low and what there was tended to concentrate increasingly in the upper class. Government finance was even worse; it may shock conservative economists of today to learn that one of Rome's troubles was that it had no national debt. Extraordinary expenditures such as a war had to be paid for by a capital levy—contributions in money or materials from the

rich, in forced labor from the poor, of the provinces
where the operations were going on; and as war, foreign
or civil, became the rule rather than the exception, all
provinces found their resources eaten away. In such
straits the Emperors could think of no expedient but de-
basement of the currency; which, once begun, went on
and on. Gradually inflation destroyed the fortunes of
the middle class; but old laws requiring Senators to in-
vest part of their fortunes in Italian real estate had
turned this millionaire class into a landed aristocracy.
Inflation meant only that their income was increasingly
in kind, not in money; as middle-bracket rich men were
impoverished Senatorial fortunes were not materially
reduced; and when all other taxable values were vanishing, most Senators regarded every attempt to increase
their taxes as little better than treason to the state.

No wonder that in such a world old ideas and ideals
were losing their power, that there was a growing loss of
faith and fortitude; that more and more people were
finding solace in salvation religions which offered com-
pensation hereafter for miseries inevitable here below.

III

In that world Gallienus grew up, and in the best of
that world; his father, Publius Licinius Valerianus, was
a wealthy and cultured Senator. Of the remoter back-

ground of the family we know nothing; it may have been descended from the republican Licinii, but in the third century when personal nomenclature was increasingly various and picturesque so thoroughly old-Roman a name as Licinius Valerianus raises the suspicion of an enfranchised provincial not very far back in the ancestry, perhaps even a manumitted slave. But certainly by the time Gallienus was born the family was rich and prominent, and Valerian seems to have shared the ideas and the viewpoint of his class. It is only a guess that his wife Egnatia Mariniana may have been responsible, whether by heredity or by influence, for the utterly anachronistic realism and originality of their son.

Realism, in those days, was not comfortable; for it was obvious to anyone who kept his eyes open that the Roman world was slipping downhill. Barbarians kept swarming over the frontiers, and were thrown back with increasing difficulty; the Persians, dreaming of the recovery of irredentas, of their historical claim to the empire of Darius, attacked and were repulsed—but with increasing difficulty; Emperor after Emperor was set up by the army, and by the army—his own or some other ambitious general's—was presently pulled down. Gallienus was seventeen when the army for the first time draped the purple cloak on a man of its own kind, Maximinus the Thracian, who has come down in our sources as a real proletarian leader—but a sort of

Pancho Villa, with no policy beyond exploiting the exploiters. Some modern historians have tried to maintain that he was a far-sighted strategist; that if he plundered the rich, it was because he knew the money was needed for counter-offensives against the Germans. But most of the money seems to have stuck to the soldiers' fingers; and whatever his purposes, his methods provoked a counter-revolution in which for the last time not only the rich and well-born, but all the civilized urban classes, rose up together against a hill-billy army and an Emperor who embodied its appetites and resentments. Maximinus was assassinated; but the two gentlemen ("Emperors in name, Consuls in spirit," G. P. Baker calls them) whom the Senate had elected in his place were presently overthrown too, and the crown again became a football for the armies to kick around. After the fall of Maximinus the troops did not again attempt to set a promoted top sergeant at the head of the empire; their generals were Senators and they proclaimed first one general and then another—perhaps hoping that each would be better than his predecessor at giving them what they wanted; perhaps not knowing what they wanted, sure of nothing except that whatever was, was wrong.

No modern can make much sense of this endless succession of mutinies and revolutions that ran through the two-thirds of a century from the murder of Caracalla to the accession of Diocletian. Rostovtzeff tries to explain it as a blind, unconscious class struggle—the soldiers who came from the underprivileged classes blunder-ingly expressing the resentment of their kind, in the only way they knew, against those who were enjoying the good things of life. But the poor suffered too from these incessant civil wars, suffered probably more than the rich; and there was the continuing complication of barbarian invasions, hordes of Goths or Franks or Ale-manni swarming over every frontier left vacant when its defenders went off for their March to Rome. Class feeling doubtless played a part; but there was, as is ap-parent in reverse from the optimistic propaganda in-scriptions on the coinage of one Emperor after another, a general recognition that things were going badly, a persistent conviction that it was the fault of the man at the top, whoever he might be; a faith—almost the only faith in terrene matters still surviving—that some-body else, anybody else, could do a better job.

It is worth remarking that every one of these third-century Emperors, no matter what his antecedent record, no matter how he got to the top, did the best job he could; there is perhaps no other instance in history of so long a succession of men rising, to the best of their abilities, to a responsibility which was beyond any man's power. And they must have been pretty certain, toward the end at least, that their reward would be nothing but assassination; in seventy years only two Emperors died natural deaths, and both after very brief reigns. Sometimes it seems that the inevitable rebellions or conspiracies against every Emperor, aristocrat or roughneck, able man or incompetent, sprang from no intelligible motives at all, represented a mere mass neurosis that had seized on the soldiery.

The man who was made Emperor by a military revolt in the year 249 happened to be a gentleman of the old school named Gaius Messius Traianus Decius, a representative of the ideas dominant in the Senate, who thought he knew what the country needed and was determined to set right whatever had been mismanaged by his predecessors, men too lily-fingered for their job. It seemed to Decius that the faith of the fathers and the fabric of society were alike being undermined by a subversive alien ism, and that the most crying need of the times was the extirpation of Christianity. To a man of his type it was unthinkable that Christianity might be a symptom rather than a cause, and he set to the work of persecution with characteristic energy and resolution. He seems to have been aided in this as in other parts of his program by Valerian, the father of Gallienus; a dozen years earlier Valerian had already stood forth as a leader of conservative opinion, he had been active in the counter-revolution against Maximinus; and now his views concurred so thoroughly with those of Decius that he became the Emperor's most trusted adviser and assistant.

The Decian persecution was by far the greatest danger the Church had ever had to face. It did indeed render Christianity an indirect service by distinguishing the die-hard confessors, faithful even before the lions in the arena, from the fair-weather brethren who lapsed in the face of danger; but even this discrimination caused the Church a good deal of trouble later, when the storm had blown over and the penitents wanted to return to the fold. The principal expert on persecution of our day says that an idea can never be extirpated by force unless that force is used in the service of another idea, and Decius's only idea seems to have been a return to the good old days and to the virtues, now somewhat superannuated, that had made the forefathers great; but he did the Church great damage and might have done far more if he had not been distracted, after a year or so, by the greatest German invasion that Rome had ever yet suffered—the first mass incursion of the Goths.

The Germans of that day were less sophisticated than their current descendants. They did not talk of the need of more *Lebensraum* for the Gothic nation, they did not justify themselves with elaborate theories of *Geopolitik* and *Grossraumswirtschaft;* they did not even pretend that their *Volksgenossen* across the border were being atrociously abused by the degenerate and non-Aryan

Romans. They merely saw some loot they wanted, and went after it. And they were a very different lot, it might be added, from their nearer descendants who under Alaric and Theodoric overran the western empire. Third-century Goths seem to have wanted only to plunder and destroy the Mediterranean civilization; fifth-century Goths, Christianized and exposed for two hundred years to Roman influence, asked for nothing more than to be allowed to join it. To the men who postponed that conquest for two centuries, our debt is inestimable.

Decius had not the fortune to be one of them. He went to meet the Goths, who were looting the Danube provinces, richer then than they have ever been since; but for all his courage and resolution he had far less skill as a strategist than the Gothic king (or *Oberster Feldherr*) Cniva. After two summers of fighting with varying fortune, a war which of course was unvaryingly ruinous to the civilian population, Decius was trapped and killed with most of his army.

Why his successor, set up by the troops of course, did not take the precaution of liquidating Valerian, who had been Decius's right-hand man and was now the outstanding representative of Decius's ideas, is not clear; perhaps he was afraid of alienating Senatorial opinion, and the opinion of the city of Rome which was chiefly created by the Senate; or perhaps he merely thought that

Valerian was too old to be dangerous. At any rate the father of Gallienus remained in high office; and after another mutiny and assassination, and then another, Publius Licinius Valerianus—at the age of seventy— became head of the Roman state.

IV

He was a skilful politician—skilful enough to postpone for some years resumption of persecution of the Christians, at a time when the peoples of the empire were suffering so much from without that they needed as much interior peace as they could get; he had a talent for civil administration which in the third century B. C. would have made him a useful servant of the republic. But the third century A. D. was no time to entrust the empire to an old man of little military experience and no military capacity. He was important only as an embodiment of the views of that wealthy and educated class which still provided the governors of provinces and the commanders of armies—which is to say that it also provided the Emperors, as well as the unsuccessful pretenders to the throne; and which still believed, as a class, that all the country needed was a chief executive who would keep taxes down, and stamp out those alien doctrines that were debilitating the rugged self-reliance of the early days of the republic.

At least Valerian knew that he needed help on his job, and he wanted to provide for the succession; so he promptly persuaded the Senate to elect his son Gallienus, then thirty-five years old, as his colleague—Emperor with full powers and privileges, but a junior and subsidiary Emperor. So long as Valerian lived he was head of the state, and for the next seven years it suffered from his incompetence. The historian Zosimus, always inclined to see merit in the enemies of Christianity, could find nothing better to say for Valerian than that he meant well. In civil affairs he seems to have been tolerably successful—as successful as anyone could be when the empire was pounded by annual invasions on all frontiers, and was rotten with plague and famine inside; but civil affairs were in those days of secondary importance. Zonaras sums up the situation in a phrase whose literal import is more exactly expressive than its common implication of general troublesomeness—*enochloumenon ton pragmaton,* things were crowding in.

Franks and Alemanni were breaking through the Rhine defenses, the Goths each year swarmed over the Danube; some of them had taken to the sea, and were plundering the coasts of Asia Minor. The Persians, crusading to redeem the lost provinces, were striking deep into Syria and Anatolia. It was no time for an Emperor to stay in Rome—especially as any victorious army commander was likely to be set up by his enthusiastic troops, whether he liked it or not, as a claimant to the throne. Yet for some years Valerian, too old for active campaigning if he could avoid it, did stay in Rome, sending Gallienus to the front; and at a moment when every front needed attention, Gallienus decided that the Rhine was the most important.

Most Romans of his day would have selected the Danube; in that quarter the barbarians had been most successful and had done most damage; and the Danube provinces were conspicuously worth saving because they provided the best soldiers in the empire—the Illyrians, ancestors of the modern Albanians, who were on the way to becoming the dominant caste in the army. It is the first known instance of Gallienus's insight that he perceived that Gaul, the bridgehead of civilization in northern Europe, was more important still. He went to Gaul, drove out the Franks and Alemanni, allies who never dreamed that they would one day give new names to hostile countries on opposite sides of the Rhine; and for seven years he kept them out. It could have been no easy task, with an army which he found undisciplined and disorganized; but he made it a little easier by making an alliance with one German tribe, the Marcomanni, against the rest. To cement the alliance he married the chief's daughter, Pipa. Gallienus had a wife already, Cornelia Salonina; and though Roman law recognized concubinage and made divorce easy it knew nothing of legitimate bigamy. But that was no time to stand on technicalities, if a tribe of Germans could be brought over to the Roman side.

Gaul had been saved, but at the cost of abandoning the Danube provinces to the Goths; none of Valerian's generals could stop them. (So, at least, it seems; all the history of that time must be reconstructed from wretchedly untrustworthy materials, and while the broad outline is visible experts differ on almost every detail.) Worse than that, the Persians were gradually absorbing Syria; they had taken and sacked Antioch, third city of the empire, had gone home with their plunder and were getting ready to come back again. Valerian, at last, had to go east. Knowing his own limitations he picked a good general as his chief of staff— Successianus, who had beaten off the Goths on the Black Sea. But the army of Syria was disorderly, insubordinate, disinclined to fight; troops as well as the civilian population were decimated by the plague that had broken out in Decius's day and had been raging ever since. When Successianus left the Black Sea front the Goths broke in; and in Syria, he and Valerian accomplished nothing.

Nothing, that is, against the Persians. But just as the Nazis, before they were strong enough to lick anybody else, nourished their self-esteem now and then by a resounding victory over the Jews, so Valerian compensated for his inability to beat the Persians by turning on the Christians. The legal ground for persecution, then as earlier, was refusal to burn incense on the altar of the Emperor, or to sacrifice to the traditional gods for the Emperor's welfare—the ancient equivalent of modern refusal to salute the flag for conscience' sake; and then as now, there were men who thought that a perfunctory gesture made under compulsion of the police would engender patriotism and promote the welfare of the state. Yet Valerian showed more dexterity than had Decius; instead of a root-and-branch drive against the whole body of communicants he arrested and executed bishops, forbade church services and burials, sabotaged the machinery of the Church with a minimum of effort and trusted to Nature to take its course with the mass of believers. Local feeling sometimes carried persecution further, however; in a time of universal misery, plague and famine and disaster, it was natural to blame the misfortunes of the empire on a sect that denied and blasphemed its gods; and it was as safe and easy then to take everything out on the Christians as it has been, in subsequent centuries, to take it out on the Jews.

Yet the persecution must have done considerable damage to the social order, and to the loyalty of the populace, in Syria and Anatolia where Christianity was rela-

tively strong; and these were just the regions threatened
by the Persians. They came back again; Valerian lost
a battle and tried negotiations; and he was trapped and
made captive by Sapor the Persian King. There is not
much use now in trying to find out which, if any, of the
conflicting versions of the circumstances is the true
one; or how much fact, if any, underlies the later and
highly embellished legends of his mistreatment at
Sapor's hands. All we know is that he was taken prisoner, and died in captivity.

V

This happened in 260. Nine years earlier a Roman
Emperor, for the first time, had been killed in action;
now for the first time a Roman Emperor had suffered
the disgrace of being captured by an enemy. It was the
climactic disaster of a catastrophic time; the Persians
had taken Antioch again and were thrusting far up into
Asia Minor; barbarians were burning and looting all the
way from Transylvania down to the Aegean; Gaul and
Italy itself were with difficulty defended against German raids, the civilized regions of Africa were being
wasted by desert tribes; taxes and prices were high, trade
and commerce had come to a standstill, plague and
famine lay heavy on the whole empire; and any man
who had money, even any peasant who had food, was

likely to be robbed of it by passing soldiers—defenders of the people as burdensome to the people as the invaders they were supposed to fight. As power had gradually become centralized, so had responsibility; whoever was Emperor was blamed for everything that went wrong. Valerian was now beyond reach, but there was left Gallienus to take the blame—Gallienus far away in the northwest, whom the bulk of the empire had never seen.

No wonder that rebellions broke out everywhere. The army of the East, rallying as the Persians scattered to loot, won some local successes; and then when the Persians were on their way home the troops set up new Emperors and started toward Rome to install them in the capital. Other pretenders had sprung up, or been thrust up, on the Danube, in Greece, in Egypt; everywhere the local troops were acclaiming their local commander as the successor to Gallienus the Unlucky. Particularist tendencies had long been in evidence both east and west; now it began to seem that the empire which held the Mediterranean world together might disintegrate into a collection of disunited states, none of them strong enough to resist the Goths or the Persians.

But already Gallienus was on his way east.

He had started, apparently, as soon as he could after he learned of his father's disaster, leaving his half-grown son as nominal commander in Gaul with an able

officer named Silvanus to do the work for him; and
he was taking with him the most efficient Roman army
that had been seen since the days of Septimius Severus.
Gallienus had realized that the day when Rome could
rely on frontier garrisons had gone by; what was
needed was a highly mobile force of shock troops. He
had used his respite in Gaul, after the frontiers had
been reestablished, to build up a cavalry army—Dal-
matian lancers in full armor, Moorish javelin throwers,
perhaps mounted archers from Mesopotamia too. This
force had been organized and trained, and put under
command of an able Illyrian officer named Aureolus;
and now it was to be tested. Gallienus took it east—but
before he had got very far he learned that even Gaul,
which he had rescued and reorganized, had turned
against him.

The troops left there had beaten back some German
raiders and recovered their loot; Postumus, commander
at Cologne, wanted to let the soldiers keep it; Silvanus,
acting for Gallienus, wanted to turn it into the treasury.
This was no mere gesture of avarice; nor was it probably, as has been suggested, inspired by the visionary
hope of being able to sort out the property and give it
back to the people from whom it had been taken. In
those days when no commander could trust any troops
that were out of his sight, he had to keep his money
with him, or anything that could be turned into money.

The treasury's gold reserve had gone east with Gallienus, and the headquarters in Gaul may well have been short of funds. But the soldiers, disappointed of their plunder, mutinied and killed Silvanus and the Emperor's son. They proclaimed Postumus Emperor in Gaul, and Spain and Britain went over to him; about all that Gallienus had left was the shock troops—and the skill to use them.

On his way east he seems to have paused (so far as the confused chronology can be reconstructed) to throw another German army out of northern Italy; then he went on to the Danube where a pretender barred his way, but Aureolus and the cavalry put that pretender down. Gallienus pushed on, then, hoping to reconstruct the eastern front; but a second revolt broke out in the Balkans behind him. The Emperor, already at Byzantium, had to turn back; and by the time that rival was overthrown Italy needed attention once more. While Gallienus was driving out another batch of Germans, and pursuing them across the Alps, and repairing the fortresses on the northern border, the army of the East came into the Balkan countries, bringing their pair of home-made Emperors with them; and the Illyrian legions, still resentful at Gallienus's long neglect of their home country, revolted for the third time within a year and joined the Orientals. Consider for a moment how this must have felt to the man who was responsible for

everything and in a time of universal panic and despair
was blamed for everything; who knew that there were
situations, east and west, that needed immediate attention but yet who could not move without seeing something that he had thought was going to stay put giving
way behind him.

But Aureolus and the cavalry again had the situation
well in hand; a little fighting and the Orientals sur-
rendered, and another pair of pretenders was out of the
way. The governor of Greece had also proclaimed himself Emperor but "within a short time," says his biographer, "he was killed by his own soldiers"—an obituary
that would serve for most of the generals of that century.
Egypt too had seceded, but Gallienus somehow managed to scrape together an expeditionary force that
landed in Alexandria and brought the Egyptians back
into the union. . . . And after the most terrible year that
the Roman Empire had ever known, a year in which it
seemed that a thousand-year-old culture was vanishing
in utter deliquescence, men began to realize that the
end of all things had not quite come, after all. Gallienus
was still in the driver's seat, and he was driving.

Symptomatic is the change of heart of the Illyrian
legions. They were supposed to be the best troops in the
empire, they had risen against Gallienus three times in
quick succession; and three times he or his subordinates
had slapped them down. Understandably, they felt

that a man who could do that must be pretty good; they were devoted to him, for the rest of his lifetime. So the Germans had been driven out, the pretenders had been crushed; Gallienus was in undisputed control of Italy and Africa and Egypt, and the Balkan provinces. He had had no time to take care of the eastern front, but it had begun to take care of itself. Odenathus the Arab prince of Palmyra, on the edge of the desert, had been half inclined to throw in with the Persians; but, insulted by the Great King as Eugene of Savoy was later insulted by Louis XIV, he proved no less vindictive. He delivered an effective counterstroke against the Persians on their way home, and now he was holding the frontier. Gallienus let him hold it; for there was still Gaul and the West to be recovered from Postumus.

There was also, in Gaul, a son to be avenged, but in the East there was a father to be avenged; from what we know of Gallienus it was chiefly the insight of a strategist and statesman that turned him westward. Yet it seems that he had never got along very well with his father—or perhaps rather with his senior colleague in the empire; their natures, their fundamental convictions, their approaches to every problem were irreconcilably different. When he heard of Valerian's capture Gallienus had remarked, "I knew that my father was mortal"; which, in Gibbon's opinion, evinced a savage coldness. But it may perhaps have been only the un-

guarded expression of his first emotion—the feeling of
a man with a genius for administration, a man maddeningly conscious of what had to be done, who for years
had been unable to do it because his father clung stubbornly to outgrown ways and to objectives no longer
attainable.

Gaul had to be recovered but Gallienus knew that a
civil war between two Roman army groups was a luxury Rome could ill afford, so he challenged Postumus
to a duel, a man-to-man single combat for the supreme
power. "I," returned Postumus frigidly, "am not a
gladiator"; but he knew Gallienus and his reply may
have been inspired by prudence as much as by dignity.
Now the armies had to fight it out instead; Gallienus
won a great victory and might have ended the war—
but that Aureolus, pursuing with the cavalry, let Postumus escape. Most of the Emperor's friends believed
that Aureolus had been bought, and ultimately it looked
as if they had been right; but Gallienus could not believe
it—perhaps dared not believe it, of his best fighting
general. Another battle, another victory; the routed
Postumus was shut up in a city—but in the siege Gallienus was badly wounded, and his army had no appetite
for fighting when he was on his back. This simple fact
is perhaps as good a testimonial to his quality as can
be found. With him the troops could always win; without him, at that time, they would not even try. The at-

tempt to recover Gaul and restore the unity of the
empire—a major war, quite as costly in lives and money
as any campaign against the Goths or Persians—had
failed, and could not soon be resumed.

Whatever might be said against Postumus, he was a
Roman and an able soldier; he could be counted on to
defend the Rhine frontier. Odenathus on the opposite
side of the empire was an Oriental, touchy and unsta-
ble; he could no more dream of becoming Roman Emperor than an Indian Rajah could dream of becoming
King of England (though his widow dreamed it after-
ward for her son) but if he changed sides the whole
East was lost. None, perhaps, of Gallienus's feats was
more brilliant than his adroit handling of this difficult
ally. He perceived, correctly, that if Odenathus were
appointed a Roman general, if he were heaped with
titles and honors just short of the Emperor's own, he
could be trusted to defend the eastern provinces against
the Persians. East and west the situation, if not satisfactory, was for the moment safe; and here in the cen-
ter, while the Germans were getting their breaths for
a fresh attack, Gallienus could begin the reconstruction
that was imperatively needed, if the Roman world was
to withstand the next shock.

To signalize at least the momentary restoration of
order, and to gratify the Roman crowd that still expected the Emperor to give it a good show, he celebrated

the tenth anniversary of his accession with great splendor. In the triumphal procession that was part of the display marched prisoners taken on all fronts, including even a few Persians. When these came along some local wits ran up and down the line studying each man's face, and when somebody asked them what they were doing they replied, "We're looking for the Emperor's father." . . . The story later told by a hostile historian that Gallienus had the wise-crackers burnt alive is thoroughly improbable; he was not that kind of man. But eccentric though he was, uncongenial as he may have found his father, he could not have enjoyed the joke very much. It was a reminder, not only to a son but to an Emperor, of things that had been left undone.

VI

There were things that could be done, and in this interlude of peace—four years, as nearly as we can determine—he began to do them. He went on with his military reforms, building his New Model army on a substructure of the old legions, picking out able officers—Illyrians, most of them, Aureolus, Claudius, Aurelian—for the high commands. He strengthened the navy—long neglected and badly needed, now that the Goths had annexed the Greek maritime states of the Crimea and were using their fleets for invasion by sea.

He began refortifying ports and cities that had lain undefended in the long Roman peace, but could no longer be left unprotected against the next barbarian incursion.

Above all he began an administrative reform, military and civil, that soon made him the best hated man in Rome. The Senate had given grudging acquiescence, nearly three centuries earlier, to the constitutional amendments of Augustus, because Augustus had taken care to reserve most of the good jobs in the government for Senators; and ever since they had been filled by Senators—members of a class that had changed immensely in provenance and background, had expanded from a group of well-born families in a single city till it represented the plutocracy of the whole empire; but had never lost its stubborn conviction that its members, whoever they might be, had a right to the juiciest plums. Gallienus had been born and bred in that class; he knew it through and through and he had realized that it no longer had any force left—nor any ideas, except a blind and futile clinging to time-honored ways and time-honored privileges. Such contributions as proud and cultured gentlemen might have made to civil government, even in the days of the Antonines, were of minor value now; what was needed was men who were adapted to changed times, who knew what it was all about—soldiers, whom the men under their command could trust. Which meant professional army men, not wealthy amateurs who commanded legions in the interval between civilian offices; and professional army men in those days had mostly come up from the ranks—ex-centurions, promoted roughnecks who understood the emotions of the buck private because they had once been buck privates themselves.

So gradually Gallienus began excluding Senators from military commands, and to a considerable degree from the provincial governorships which usually implied military command; filling each appointment, as it fell vacant, with a self-made man who looked as if he could handle the job. He must have known that he would be damned as a traitor to his class—damned not only in the continuing tradition of the Senatorial aristocracy, but in the popular feeling of Rome which reflected Senatorial sentiment, in the literary tradition which depended on an ever-narrowing educated class. He must have known, but there is no evidence that he cared; he was not the sort of man to worry about what posterity was going to think of him.

And he had to deal with the Christian menace. It could not then be foreseen that the Church would eventually make a compromise with the World; in theory Christianity was totalitarian and revolutionary, and no wonder old-school conservatives such as Decius and Valerian had concluded that the only way to deal with it was to root it out. But they had not succeeded in rooting it out; and Gallienus seems to have perceived not only that this method was unprofitable, but that Christianity lived through persecutions because it satisfied some people's longings as nothing else could do. So he not only stopped the persecutions, but restored the confiscated churches and cemeteries—a milestone in ecclesiastical history, for now at last what had in legal theory been an illicit underground organization gained official recognition of its right to exist; and, having done that, he set himself to find and popularize a moral and emotional substitute for Christianity.

He picked the wrong one—the only time, so far as we know, that he betrayed the characteristic failing of his class and looked backward. Devoted to the old Greek culture—rather in the mood, it seems, of our sentimental medievalists—encouraging an artistic renaissance that attempted to go back, if not to classic at least to Hellenistic models, he used the considerable powers of propaganda that an Emperor could command to try to spread the cult of Demeter of Eleusis. (This seems to have been the origin of those coins on which he pictured himself, in the dress of the goddess, under the title of "the Empress Galliena"—a publicity release interpreted most adversely to his reputation in later ages which failed to comprehend some of the religious ideas of the third century. The concept of a comprehensive, and consequently bisexual divine element becomes more intelligible now that an influential sect speaks of our Father-Mother-God, with much ontological justification.) The Demeter-worship seems, from what little we know of it, to have been a salvation cult of a rather austere type—too austere, it turned out, for third-century taste. Its ritual dramatized the same doctrine as the ritual of Masonry, and may have had the emotional effect that Masonic ritual can have, even on initiates who are skeptical of the doctrine; it may have looked like the best adapted of time-honored religions to the needs of the day. But it was not enough for men and women who felt that all they had known was crumbling under them. The army, then and for decades later, was devoted to the Unconquered Sun; the women still worshipped Isis; and there was an increasing drift to Christianity which had incorporated, or was soon to incorporate, the most attractive features of both its rivals.

Gallienus knew that Demeter would not do for the educated classes; but he hoped that they might find an emotional focus in Neoplatonism. How far he was personally given to its doctrines nobody can say; his wife Salonina was a disciple of Plotinus, and her devotion may have reinforced her husband's calculated conviction that here was the strongest rallying point for a revival of the ancient culture. Plotinus's biographer Porphyry tells us that Gallienus used to talk of turning over a ruined city in Campania to the philosopher, who could there try to organize a Platonic republic. But it is just conceivable that this may have seemed the politest way to get Plotinus off the premises, to keep him from hanging around the Palatine and talking philosophy when there was work to be done.

It was quite a brisk little renaissance, while it lasted, with the Emperor himself as its leader; his most hostile biographer cannot deny that "he was renowned in oratory, in poetry, and in all the arts." When Gallienus died his renaissance died with him; perhaps that endeavor was hopeless, demanding a vitality which Graeco-Roman culture had lost. But the ambition to reunite the empire was not hopeless. Postumus, it had been proved, could be beaten, whenever the state could afford another civil war; Odenathus's widow Zenobia was behaving almost as an independent sovereign in the East, but Gallienus's shock troops had proved that they could beat the Syrian army too. The separate governments in East and West were clear indications of a tendency to fission, which later Emperors recognized and regularized; but there were centripetal tendencies as well, there was already the feeling—which persisted clear through the Dark Ages—that however administration might be divided, Romania was all one piece. Given a few years more to rebuild, Gallienus could probably have done what Aurelian did after him. But he never had the chance to try it; for the Goths came back.

VII

They came by sea, in 267—coasting around the Black
Sea, ravaging the shores of Asia Minor far down toward
the Mediterranean. Why Gallienus failed to stop them
we do not know; but, given his character, it is probable
that he was occupied with some nearer and more urgent
war; and in view of what happened the next year we
may infer that it was a defensive war against Postumus,
who was no longer content with the western quarter of
the empire, but wanted it all. So the Goths went triumphantly home, with so much loot that all the tribes
decided to go in for Viking-faring. And the next spring
they came back again, in greater numbers than ever before, by land and by sea.

Gallienus's fleet stopped their naval contingent before it got into the Aegean, but on land he was too late
to head them off—again, most probably, because he had
to see that Italy was safe from Postumus before he left.
The Gothic torrent flowed through Thrace and down
into Greece; Athens was plundered. But there the fleet
met the invaders, landed marines, helped the home
guard drive out the Goths; and as they drifted home-
ward through the Balkan peninsula Gallienus was there
to intercept them.

The cavalry general Aureolus, ablest of his subordinates, had been left behind in charge of Italy, and part of the cavalry with him. Commanding the cavalry of the expeditionary force in his place was another Illyrian, Aurelian—a general risen from the ranks by headlong energy and reckless courage; in an army which by now included no soft characters he was a conspicuously tough person, they called him Hand-on-Sword. The infantry with Gallienus included the Praetorian Guard under a certain Heraclian, and probably Illyrian legions, since the Illyrian Claudius was second in command. They met the Germans at Nish, and overwhelmingly defeated them; the remnant of the invaders fled to a nearby mountain, barricaded themselves behind their covered wagons, and were shut in. Nothing remained but to sit there and starve them out, and the Danube provinces would be freed at last from the Gothic fury which had raged for fifteen years. We know it could have been done because it was done, the next year, by other men who finished the job planned and half accomplished by Gallienus. But before he could finish it he heard the worst news of his career. Aureolus who had been his Stonewall Jackson had sold out to Postumus; he was still holding Italy—but holding it for the rival Emperor in Gaul.

"When it was necessary," says even the hostile biographer of Gallienus, "he was swift, forceful, impetuous"; and it was necessary now. Leaving part of his

forces to watch the blockaded Germans, he hurried back
to Italy. Aureolus was the best general in the army and
had some of the best troops; he had won brilliant vic-
tories and may very well have regarded himself as the
man who had really made Gallienus. But when Gallienus met him Aureolus was licked, like everybody else
who ever met Gallienus in open battle. The surviving
rebels fled into Milan, and Gallienus sat down to be-
siege them. . . . But in sieges, he never had any luck.
Wounded at a siege in Gaul, he had had to let Postumus
go; his siege of the Germans on the mountain had been
interrupted by the revolt of Aureolus; and now as he
besieged Aureolus, whom he once had trusted, the
men he still trusted put their heads together and decided
that Gallienus had lived long enough.

Claudius, Aurelian, Heraclian, men he had picked
out and promoted to the highest commands—it is pretty
clear that they were all in the conspiracy, even though
subsequent apologists tried to whitewash them. What
were their motives? The twentieth-century mind cannot with confidence try to comprehend third-century
reasoning, when the fine art of double-crossing had
been developed to a point not reached again till the
Renaissance. It is tempting to regard the third-century
Roman army as nothing but a gang of mobsters on a
grand scale, making the public pay for a protection
which it did not always get; and its generals as gang

leaders, uneasily suspicious of one another, waiting for their chance to rub out the Big Guy at the top. In certain aspects things were indeed like that; but the situation was far more complex and so must be any valid explanation.

In this particular conspiracy the Senate certainly had a hand; for Claudius had been selected to replace Gallienus and during his brief reign he showed himself the Senate's man. He was a man of ability and patriotism, by the curious standards of the time; but he was an Illyrian hick—a homespun statesman of the kind that has often been won over to a reactionary program by social attention from members of the best clubs; and an Illyrian hick who would do what he was told to do would suit the Senate far better than a Roman gentleman who was a traitor to his class. They were all Illyrians, these leaders of the conspiracy—all roughnecks risen from the ranks. Perhaps they resented Gallienus's breeding, his intellectuality, his versatile talents which could be envied even by men who were not equipped to appreciate them. And not impossibly his eccentric temperament, his acrid and sometimes recondite humor, his contempt for irrelevancies combined with a passionate interest in what must have seemed irrelevancies to Balkan mountaineers, made him hard to get along with in day-by-day contact. Cruder men could feel his superiority even if they could not comprehend it, knew that he was aware of it even though he never flaunted it; quite conceivably he rubbed them the wrong way.

Moreover, the Illyrians were still the backbone of the army; Illyrian generals may have felt that the troops would rather have a man of their own race and their own kind on the throne. Gallienus, after all, had concluded that the situation necessitated the removal of all gentlemen from the public service, with a single exception— Gallienus himself. Why not be consistent and remove him too? (Gallienus would have appreciated the sour humor of that reasoning, if he had lived.) And finally, he had everything but luck; and bad luck in those days was generally regarded as a sign of the disfavor of the gods. They were all sun worshippers, these conspirator-generals, and so were most of their men; untainted by classical culture, all they knew about Demeter of Eleusis was that she had not gone over, she was not what the public wanted. Gallienus had picked the wrong god and the other gods had no use for him; get rid of him, then, and make room for a man whose god was strong.

So there was a night alarm in the camp of the besiegers outside Milan; Gallienus, headlong as ever, leaped out of bed and ran out of his tent, unarmored, to see what was happening; and a javelin—"it was not certain whose, in the darkness"—struck him down. His sons who had accompanied him were murdered too; his wife, who was also with him, seems to have been spared. But when his fellow club members in Rome heard the joyful news, they promptly butchered all the rest of the family.

Meanwhile the conspirators had experienced an awful disillusionment. The army, which ought to have been so gratified at the replacement of a Roman gentleman by a Balkan mountaineer, rose up in mutiny, lamenting the loss of an Emperor "who was useful, brave, and necessary—who got things done." Luckily there was at hand an argument which Roman soldiers of those days could never resist. Gallienus always traveled accompanied not only by his family but, as noted above, by the treasury gold reserve. The conspirators had it now; twenty pieces of gold hastily handed out to each soldier proved an efficacious sedative; the story spread by the conspirators that Gallienus, as he lay dying had nominated Claudius as his successor was swallowed with whatever qualms; and thus Claudius the Second became Emperor of Rome.

Like every man who in those days grasped the power or had it thrust upon him, he lived up to his responsibility. He stayed where he was and finished Aureolus; then he went back into the Balkans and finished the Goths, so thoroughly that they did not again become a serious danger for more than a century. After that, the plague took him off; and the Senate, deluded by his

friendliness into the conviction that it was once more
the fountain-head of authority, elected his brother in
his place. But Aurelian—old Hand-on-Sword—decided
to elect himself; the moment he came out for the office
the soldiers abandoned the Senate's candidate; and Senators who had been moved to murderous rage by the
failure of one of their own kind to pay them proper attention discovered that they were in the power of a hard-
fisted Balkan soldier, who did not think it was worth
while to pay them any attention at all. Hard-fisted
Balkan soldiers ruled Rome for the next century; the
Senate retained a sort of Social-Register prestige, but
nothing more.

Aurelian, in the five years he ruled before he was
murdered (by his own men, naturally) recovered Gaul
and brought the Oriental secessionists back into the
union; finding time in between to repel two great and
dangerous German invasions of Italy and to put down
an insurrection in Rome. He called himself Restorer
of the World and he had earned the title, but his in-
strument was the army that Gallienus had made. Claudius, Aurelian, Probus—their successive efforts pulled
the disintegrating organism together again; Diocletian
and Constantine put it into working order, and thus
made Europe possible. They all deserved well of the
state, and of the future; but in almost every field, they
built on the work done by Gallienus in the hour when

heaven was falling, the day when earth's foundations
fled.

VIII

Such is the judgment of virtually all recent historians
on Gallienus—a crescendo of acknowledgment which
reaches its climax in the thoroughly documented chapters contributed by Professor Alföldi of Budapest to the
final volume of the *Cambridge Ancient History*. No
scholar myself, I have followed in the main his chronology and his interpretations—filling a gap, occasionally, by one of those plausible guesses that may be permitted to the amateur when the professional would have
to say, "Not proven." And the truth about Gallienus
deserves to be passed on to a different (and I hope
larger) public than the people who will not only buy but
read fat volumes by scholarly historians; for he got a
worse break in his publicity than almost any other figure
of ancient times.

For seventeen centuries this indefatigable worker,
this soldier and statesman of the first rank, was regarded
as the worst and most contemptible of Roman Emperors,
a classic example of indolence and incompetence. Why?
Well, for one reason, he happened to be Emperor at a
time when things were at their very worst, when three-
quarters of a century of disintegration had brought the

empire to an all-time low. We can see now that it would have gone lower still, would perhaps have gone completely to pieces, but for Gallienus; he made the upturn possible. But all that people could see in his day was that things had never been so bad before, and the man in power was blamed for the accumulated misfortunes of the time.

Nobody in those days had the leisure to write history; and when it once more became possible those histories were naturally written by educated men who by that time were for the most part either members or dependents of the Senatorial aristocracy, the men who execrated Gallienus as a traitor. Also, most of our accounts of the period seem to have taken their present form in the fourth century, after the triumph of Christianity. The bulk of the Senatorial class remained pagan long after soldier-Emperors had gone over to the new faith; and pagans of that time remembered that it was Gallienus who had first recognized and officially tolerated the pernicious sect, had let the poisonous weed grow so rank that it choked everything. (They forgot that the diligent efforts of Decius and Valerian to root it out had after all been unsuccessful.) Tolerance, in the fourth century, was not much more of a pagan than a Christian virtue.

The Christians remembered Gallienus gratefully for a few decades; but he had only let them live, and under

Emperors who themselves were Christian, who were giving the Church an increasing share of the kingdoms of this world and the glory of them, a tolerant pagan was no longer worth any gratitude. So Gallienus achieved the unique distinction of becoming obnoxious not only to the pagan but to the Christian tradition; while the aristocracy, now contemptuously disregarded by every Emperor (except in the matter of taxation, where it managed to cling to extensive exemptions) could more easily forgive slights from a Balkan soldier than from one of its own members.

These tendencies, aristocratic class feeling and the bitterness of the rear guard of paganism, converge in what is unfortunately by far our fullest source for the history of Gallienus—the collection of biographies known as the *Historia Augusta.* Into the controversy over the date, authorship and purpose of this work in the form in which we now read it—a controversy which scholars have conducted for half a century past, with such acrimony as is usually reserved for religious disputes—a layman would be foolish to enter; yet anybody professionally engaged in the critical analysis of garbled and tendentious news stories can make one or two reasonable inferences from the life of Gallienus in this collection. Ascribed to a certain Trebellius Pollio, otherwise unknown and possibly only the pseudonym of some ghost writer, it is one of the worst of the lot, whether as literature or as history; but it clearly derives from two sources, one historical and one personal, written not very long after Gallienus's time. The historical source, while it appears to have incorporated some sound tradition, was evidently much misunderstood by the final compiler; but he seems to have passed on the human-interest stuff pretty much as he found it. Since, for reasons to be noted presently, he was trying to smear Gallienus, he filled the biography with abusive interpolations; but he left in much that contradicts his own story, and as he was an inefficient propagandist it is easy to distinguish between his editorial comments and the material he took from his source.

Or rather it ought to be easy; which brings us to the worst misfortune that Gallienus's reputation ever suffered. He was the victim of one of Edward Gibbon's least excusable blunders; and the average layman who reads Roman history gets it from Gibbon, and will go on getting it from Gibbon until (if ever) the subject is treated by another man of Gibbon's stature, both as artist and as scholar. Bury, in his edition of Gibbon, corrected this slip in a footnote; but few laymen read footnotes, even Gibbon's own, unless they have enough Latin to understand the matters which he so often relegated to this discreet obscurity.

Gibbon was for his day a very great scholar; he had not had the benefit of recent critical study of the *Historia*

Augusta, and it is not his fault that a century and a half of subsequent research in epigraphy, papyrology, and numismatics—sciences very feebly cultivated, in his time—has necessitated revision of some of his conclusions. But Alföldi's convincing reconstruction of the last Gothic campaign is based entirely on the collation of literary sources familiar to Gibbon; and Gibbon's failure to draw the inference was the least of his oversights. He detected a glaring forgery in Pollio's biography, yet he overlooked a propaganda purpose equally glaring. Pollio, or whoever provided some of his source material, wrote after Constantius Chlorus had been appointed assistant Emperor by Diocletian. This rising man, whose son was to rise still higher, had (as Don Marquis once put it) no ancestors to speak of, and wanted some ancestors to speak of; and since he was an Illyrian from the same neighborhood as the Emperor Claudius, he pretended some sort of relationship to this renowned figure. (That it was no more than pretense is suggested by the variety of relationships recorded by different historians.) Men who wrote under Constantius, still more those who revised earlier works after Constantine became sole Emperor, thus had an incentive to glorify the reputed ancestor; and to make Claudius, whose reign had been creditable but brief, look better they had to make Gallienus look worse.

Gibbon missed that, and summed up Gallienus in

a sentence which is likely to outlast the *Cambridge Ancient History*, or any other of the modern works that are sounder but duller than the *Decline and Fall:* "In every art that he attempted, his lively genius enabled him to succeed; and as his genius was destitute of judgment, he attempted every art except the important ones of war and government." This, for the man who put down a dozen rebellions, flung back a dozen invasions, and never lost a pitched battle in the open field; who reorganized military and civilian administration on the only practically possible basis; who began the search for a better focus for the spiritual unity of the world than the formal religion of a Latin town, and paved the way not only for Diocletian but for Constantine. How could a man like Gibbon go so far wrong? I think he was misled by his instinct as a literary artist, which in this case (as in some others) proved too strong for his caution as a historian.

He justifiably distrusted the Pollio biography; so after reproducing, and naturally improving, Pollio's picture he appends an apologetic footnote: "This singular character has, I believe, been fairly transmitted to us." I believe so too, *as a character* (when the editorial interpretations for which the evidence offers no warrant have been eliminated); there was no creative artist in the third century, or in the fourth, capable of inventing a figure so complex. Gibbon's artistic sense told him that

here was something real—the true portrait, however re-
touched, of a very peculiar man; and he too hastily
assumed that the historical material had an equal
validity.

IX

What sort of man, then? A realist, a rather grim
humorist, a man so conscious of his responsibilities that
he was contemptuous of non-essentials; a man who rose
to every occasion—yet might have been happier if there
had been no occasions to which he had to rise. "Now
that his memory has been cleared of the coating of
calumny," writes Alföldi, "even his natural failings
can hardly be discerned." I believe that one of them is
discernible, a weakness he mastered and turned into a
strength. Pollio accuses him of laziness, of effeminate
luxury. Effeminacy can hardly be imputed to a man who
was loved by a hard-boiled army (which he had boiled
himself); who would have fought Postumus single-
handed for the empire, rather than waste lives in a battle
which he must have known he would probably win;
who met his death because he was in such a hurry to get
into action that he would not stop to put on his breast-
plate. To the charge of laziness, the record of his labors
is sufficient refutation. Yet the recurrent and apparently
unmotivated references to his suddenness of movement,

his alacrity, his impetuosity suggest a man who would have liked to be lazy if he had ever had time. In private life he might have been another Petronius, who achieved fame by his indolence as did other men by their industry—yet even Petronius, as consul and proconsul, had shown himself energetic and equal to his job. Gallienus had a job far more exacting, a job that had to be done; and he forced himself to respond, against his nature, to every demand on him, with a headlong sudden vigor that made a lasting impression on his contemporaries. The last act of his life, that leap out of bed at the midnight alarm, sounds like the behavior of a man who hated to get out of bed, and had to make himself jump out if he was to get up at all.

He resembled Petronius, too, in his refined taste for the elegancies; he liked luxury when he had time for it, he liked flowers and good cookery, he liked music—the flute and the organ particularly. Of his oratory nothing remains; but that it was first-rate, at least by the standards of a decadent time, is proved by Pollio's admission. One sample of his poetry survives—a five-line epithalamium, graceful and rather melancholy; the mood of the Horation *carpe diem*—or *noctem* in this case—heightened by the emotional background of a time when the world was going to hell, and you might as well get what you could out of life while you could. (But perhaps an amateur imagines these overtones in a poem which formally is of a conventional type. Anyway, if you impute originality to any Roman poem, some scholar is likely to tell you that it is nothing but an imitation of an Alexandrian original, which of course is lost.)

For proof of his realism, look at his record. He discarded what would no longer work, built on whatever was still serviceable or could be made so. To a man of his tastes and education the company of Senators must have been more congenial, by and large, than that of Illyrian ex-sergeants; but he knew that the Illyrians could do what had to be done and that the Senators could not. He must have known too that his policies would cost him most of his friends in his own set, that the Illyrians would always find him a little alien and suspect; he could have had few intimates, and perhaps needed none.

His humor was of a type that is never popular. In the arena, a bullfighter failed ten successive times to kill his bull, but Gallienus gave him a prize anyway. "Why not?" he asked. "It isn't easy to miss a bull so often." In the dreadful year after his father's capture, when all the world was collapsing, he met the news of each fresh disaster with what seemed to some of his contemporaries an utterly irresponsible levity. When Egypt revolted, "Can't we get along without Egyptian linen?" he remarked. And when Gaul rose up behind him, "Won't the country be safe, even if we have to do without Gallic cloaks?" Levity, perhaps; but far more plausibly the instinctive reaction, in a time of appalling and endlessly recurrent calamities, of a man who was responsible for the safety of the civilized world, and knew better than anybody else how close it was to ruin. He had to turn off each new disaster with a wisecrack, or else go mad. . . . There was after all another executive in a time of tremendous crisis who cracked jokes amid disaster, and was called a buffoon for so doing; his name was Abraham Lincoln.

Gallienus's apparently heartless comment on his father's disaster brought him more opprobrium than anything else he ever said. But it must be repeated that this was the perhaps unguarded remark of a realist who knew that now at last the chief obstacle to a realistic policy was out of the way; it was not the obituary comment of a son on his father, but of an executive vice-president on the incompetent head of the corporation, whose blunders might now be retrieved. Possibly Gallienus at that moment ought to have been thinking as a son and not as an executive, but that one instance is insufficient justification for Gibbon's imputation of savage coldness. In other domestic relations, at least, Gallienus was far from cold; he seems to have been devoted to his children and he loved his wife Salonina, as Pollio admits, to abandonment—*perdite dilexit*. (Such an emotion in a Roman aristocrat was a mark of changed times; in the classic days of the Republic it would have been regarded as indecorous, in the chaste privacy of the home.) But he also loved his Number Two wife, the German girl Pipa; it had been a purely political marriage yet he loved her, though not to abandonment. . . . Pipa appears to be the Old German— or Low Latin, or Proto-Aryan—phonetic equivalent of *Pfeife,* and perhaps she got her name from her habits; perhaps she was a girl who whistled. Which might explain Gallienus's fondness for her; there could not have been many people on the Palatine Hill in those days, or at Imperial Headquarters in the field, who found anything to whistle about; Pipa, no doubt too ill educated to understand the situation of the world as it was evident to Gallienus—and to Salonina—took things as they came, and cheered her husband up.

As to how Pipa got along with Salonina our sources are silent; but it may be inferred from the silence that they did get along, adequately enough and on the surface. If this was another triumph of Gallienus's diplomacy, it was perhaps a greater one than his deft handling of Odenathus; but it may be that each of his wives realized, as he did, that she had a job to do; and they both did it.

Gallienus, says Alföldi, was no type like the other Emperors of his period, but an individual. So he was, and the foregoing summary is no more than a few notes

on the material waiting for somebody who can adequately re-create him. The portrait busts give us little
help; it is hard for a clean-shaven age to perceive the
traits, good or bad, of a bearded face, especially when
it is only the narrow fringe beard fashionable in his day.
Lincoln had a beard rather like that but we take Lincoln
as he comes because we are used to him; Gallienus's
beard only makes him a little more alien and incompre-
hensible. Trying to get past the beard, you can read
in the portrait busts only single facets of a polyhedral
personality; the one in the Museo delle Terme is Gallienus giving himself up for the moment to the emotional
impression of something or other—not somebody; the
Berlin bust, in the Roman style, has a hint but no more
of the you-be-damned Gallienus who went ahead and
did what had to be done whether anybody liked it or
not.

Among scholars his standing is secure; but he may
never be rehabilitated, for an audience as large as
Gibbon's, by any artist comparable to Gibbon; there is
too much else to write about, there have been too many
brave men since Agamemnon. And it will be evident
from the notes set down here that his personality could
be adequately depicted only by an artist of high rank;
he deserves to be the central figure of a novel by Naomi
Mitchison, a novel as good as *The Corn King and the
Spring Queen*. But nobody in the British Isles is likely

to have time to write historical novels for some time to come, or even to read them; I can only hope that these remarks will come to the attention of somebody, in a continent which appears to have a future, who may some day have the power to give Gallienus due recognition. To say that he made Europe possible is perhaps, in the present state of Europe, to damn him with faint praise; but Europe made America possible, and it can still be hoped that we may be enterprising enough to live up to that opportunity. If so, we shall owe some little of our gratitude to Gallienus; for his work continueth, great beyond his knowing.